Copyright © 1980, 1984, 1988 & 2013 Omnibus Press
(A Division of Music Sales Limited)

Book design: Pearce Marchbank
Artwork: Kate Hepburn/Alison Fenton
Picture research: Jane Coke, Sue Ready, Valerie Boyd
& Mary McCartney

ISBN: 978.1.783.05183.0
Order No: OP55484

Exclusive Distributors
Music Sales Limited,
14/15 Berners Street,
London, W1T 3LJ.

Music Sales Corporation
180 Madison Avenue, 24th Floor,
New York,
NY 10016,
USA.

Macmillan Distribution Services,
56 Parkwest Drive
Derrimut, Vic 3030,
Australia.

Every effort has been made to trace the copyright holders of the
photographs in this book but one or two were unreachable. We
would be grateful if the photographers concerned would contact us.

Printed in China

A catalogue record for this book is available from the British Library.

Visit Omnibus Press on the web at www.omnibuspress.com

David Bowie Black Book

The illustrated biography by Miles & Chris Charlesworth.

David Robert Jones was born on January 8, 1947 at 40 Stansfield Road, Brixton, London SW.9. His father, Haywood Stenton Jones was a Yorkshireman working for Dr. Barnardo's Homes as a public relations officer. He was first married in 1933 to Hilda Louise Sullivan and they had a daughter, Annette. The marriage broke down during the war and by 1946, after he returned from serving in North Africa with the Eighth Army, he was already living with Margaret Mary Burns in Stansfield Road. She already had a seven year old son, Terry, and after David was born they decided to get married. Haywood had to first get divorced and eventually the first Mrs Jones filed a divorce petition against her husband in the High Court on June 26, 1947. She was given a decree nisi on the grounds of her husband's adultery. The decree became absolute on August 11, 1947 and Haywood and Margaret were free to marry, which they did a month later, on September 12, 1947. David Jones was then eight months old and now had a half sister through his father as well as a half brother through his mother.

For the first eight years of his life he lived in Stansfield Road, a short street just off the main Stockwell Road. It's a poor area now and was even poorer then, crowded with the families whose homes had been destroyed by the bombing of London.

David has spoken of it in interviews, 'I never wanted and never went hungry but I saw people deprived all around and I wanted them to have better.'

When he was eight, David and his brother Terry went to live in a farmhouse in Yorkshire with their father's brother. It was a very old building complete with a seventeenth century monk's hole built for Catholic priests to hide in during the days of persecution from the Protestants. The farmhouse was in open countryside surrounded by cattle and sheep but the boys missed London and were never really happy in the country. Two years later they returned to live with their parents in a very small, comfortable, terrace house at 4 Plaistow Grove, Bromley in the suburbs of London.

These contrasts in ways of living were described by Bowie to journalist Patrick Salvo:

'I've seen pretty well the best of both, from the terrible slum area of Brixton, with a pretty heavy Black population, to right up in the country on the farms. I've been a child through both so that both halves of it really influenced me and produced a schizoid attitude in life. I think that's what confused me.'

David went to Bromley Technical High School and it was there he had a fight with his friend George Underwood over a girl. A single punch nearly cost him the sight of one eye. Bowie described it: 'The pupil was paralysed. It started bleeding. I was in hospital for months. I was very near to losing the sight in both eyes. They operated and saved my right eye but my left eye is still very dodgy.' He was left with a paralysed pupil which, in the reflection of strong light gives the eye a feline look. One eye is blue and one grey with the one pupil much larger than the other, something which is often noticeable in photographs. He remained friends with George Underwood, however, and Underwood has since designed two of his album sleeves.

One of his earliest moves was to buy a saxophone. He admired the British sax player Ronnie Ross, and, though he was still only twelve years old, he found Ross's number in the telephone book and contacted him in order to arrange for private lessons. Another influence on his sax playing was King Curtis who he heard when his father brought home a Little Richard album.

By his mid-teens he was an accomplished player and at the school end-of-term Christmas show in 1962, David topped the bill, playing sax with his group George and the Dragons. David was already quite a hero at the school for his sax playing and the show was a great success.

5

Also on the bill was a group called The Little Ravens, featuring the 12 year old Peter Frampton whose father was a master at the school. The reason a 12 year old boy would already be familiar with the work of Ronnie Ross was that his brother Terry, being seven years older, was a great influence on his life. Terry had read Jack Kerouac and Allen Ginsberg and spent a lot of his time at the late night jazz clubs in the West End. David once spoke about Terry's influence in an interview:

'It was Terry who really started everything for me. He was into all these different Beat writers and listening to jazz musicians like John Coltrane and Eric Dolphy. While I was still at school he would go up to town every Saturday evening to listen to jazz in the different clubs and this was all happening to him when I was at a very impressionable age. He was growing his hair long and rebelling in his own way, later travelling twice around the world as a merchant seaman, while I was still dressed up in school uniform every day. It all had a big impact on me.' Terry gave him a copy of Jack Kerouac's 'On The Road'. 'That's why I bought a sax. The whole thing just fitted together so well. I wanted to be just like Sal Paradise and Dean Moriarty and I almost made it — as much as one can within the confines of Bromley.'

At school David was only good at art and athletics. He was a keen runner but when it came time for exams he only passed the General Certificate of Education, O-Level in two subjects, art and woodwork. He probably neglected his school work since by then he was already playing tenor saxophone in the evenings with a modern jazz group.

'I was in school only until I was sixteen, and, as a matter of fact was under a doctor's care during much of my youth not because I was sickly but because I was accident prone. I broke a hand and then after it healed I broke a thumb on the same hand. And this was while I was planning to be an artist.

'Then I ran over myself with an automobile. I was cranking the car with it in gear and it ran against me breaking both my legs. That time I very nearly lost my masculinity entirely and to this day have a large scar on the inner side of my leg.'

While David was in hospital recovering from his eye operation the family suffered another blow. David's brother Terry went insane and had to be committed to a mental institution. David was philosophical about this and has mentioned it in interviews. 'We go every fortnight and we take a hamper of sandwiches and apples, new shirts and fresh stuff. Take his laundry. And he's always very happy to see us but he never has anything to say. Just lies there on the lawn all day, looking at the sky.'

On leaving school he had a job as a commercial artist with an advertising agency but late nights and early mornings don't mix too well and he resigned or was fired after six months. That was the only job he ever had outside the music business. He described this brief period: 'I wanted to paint but they told me at college that I was better at design and I ended up as a commercial artist. I wasn't happy at that either. I was playing tenor sax with a group in the evenings and then I had a bust up at work and decided to leave the job and become a musician...'

One day in late 1963, David went down to his local barbershop in Bromley to get a haircut. Waiting in line were four other musicians, Bob Allen, Dick Underwood, Frank Howard and Roger Buck. David joined them and they became The King Bees, a fledgling Rhythm and Blues band of the sub-Rolling Stones type. They played pubs and local clubs but got nowhere. In those days the washing machine tycoon John Bloom was getting a lot of publicity and was known to associate with various Beatles and Stones. David wrote to him asking him to finance The King Bees. Amazingly, Bloom replied, by telegram, saying that music was not his business but referring him to agent manager Les Conn.

David telephoned Conn at once and he agreed to take them on. One of the first bookings Conn organised for them was to play at a party which John Bloom was organising to celebrate his wedding anniversary. Bowie described the gig in an interview. 'It was all a bit embarrassing. The party was very posh with many of the guests in evening dress. And we turned up in our T-shirts and jeans ready to play rhythm and blues. We really worked hard that night but many of them just ignored us and carried on talking as though we weren't there. I could feel that we weren't right for the occasion. They should have booked a more conventional type of dance band.'

David even called up the next day to apologize to Conn but Conn seemed in no way put out, in fact he had found the boys a recording contract. It was with the Vocalion-Pop label, a subsidiary of Decca mainly devoted to Rhythm and Blues and Jazz. Decca already had The Rolling Stones and with Rhythm and Blues looking as if it was to be The Next Big Thing they were seeking to consolidate their position in the market. So, as Davie Jones and the King Bees, in June 1964 their first record was released. Called 'Liza Jane' it was both written and produced and musically directed by Les Conn. On it David sings a shaky lead vocal and plays a reedy saxophone. It was decidedly not a hit.

David was now sufficiently close to the music business for him to be offered a spot on the TV show 'Gadzooks! It's All Happening' in February 1965. In fact it didn't happen because he refused their demand that he cut his 15″ hair.

Decca didn't see any reason to retain the services of young David Jones and David's next appearance on vinyl was to be through the auspices of EMI. In the nine months intervening David had lost The King Bees and joined an outfit called The Manish Boys. David's style of R&B also shifted: from sub-Rolling Stones to the organ based sound of Georgie Fame and Zoot Money, complete with imitation American accent. Following in the footsteps of The Rolling Stones, they took their name from the title of a Muddy Waters composition and chose as their first release a number first sung by Bobby 'Blue' Bland, 'I Pity The Fool'. The writing credit of Deadric Malone was a name of convenience used by Duke-Peacock Records label boss Don Robey to publish songs which he had bought outright for $5.00 from the young black musicians that used to hang around his offices in Houston, Texas.

For the 'B'-side, producer Shel Talmy used David's own composition, 'Take My Tip', a number heavily influenced by Georgie Fame, whose 'Yeh, Yeh' had been number one in the charts three months earlier. Talmy had produced an almost identical version of 'Take My Tip' two months earlier as the 'B'-side of 'Restless' by Kenny Miller. This was the first of his own songs that David recorded.

The Manish Boys went the way of The King Bees and for his next recording David was known as Davie Jones and The Lower Third. The Lower Third were a basic Mod band and had

9

1963

been playing together for some time. The lineup consisted of Dennis 'T-Cup' Taylor, 22, on lead guitar who at this point had been playing for ten years, five of them with The Lower Third, Graham Rivens, 20, on bass guitar. He had been with the The Lower Third for two years. Finally, Phil Lancaster, 22, on drums. He joined The Lower Third about the same time as Bowie showed up and had previously worked with The Dave Clark Five and done other session work. Les Conn had also been jettisoned and David was now managed by Ralph Horton who joined him after working as a roadie for The Moody Blues. Horton got them a series of six Sunday afternoon gigs at The Marquee which were being recorded and sponsored by Radio London, the pirate station. David was second billing to The High Numbers who were just about to change their name to The Who. David and The Lower Third got from gig to gig in an old diesel ambulance that they bought from the local council. In the back they had mattresses where they could get some sleep on the way back from out of town gigs or just park round the corner from a late night London gig rather than spend hours delivering everyone to their homes.

The battered white ambulance was eventually parked permanently outside The Marquee and the proprietor of the club would wake them up in the mornings with containers of hot coffee.

David described The Lower Third: 'We were too loud onstage. We used feedback and sounds and didn't play any melodies. We just pulverized the sound, which was loosely based on Tamla Motown. We had an ardent following of about a hundred Mods but when we played out of London we were booed right off the stage. We weren't very good.'

It was at one of the Radio London Marquee gigs that Kenneth Pitt first saw David. Pitt, who was to manage Bowie for five years, was looking for 'another Tommy Steele', someone who could make the transition from singing with a group and become a TV personality, West End stage star and all round entertainer. He had previously been involved with such groups as Manfred Mann and The Kinks and done publicity and international representation for such various artists as Nana Mouskouri, Anthony Newley, Judy Garland, Leonard Cohen and Nina and Frederick.

He was invited to The Marquee by David's manager, Ralph Horton, and met David soon afterwards at Horton's flat. Quite why Horton wanted to get Pitt involved is unclear but Pitt obviously knew he was going to be taking over because shortly after that, while on a business trip to New York to try and sign up Andy Warhol and The Velvet Underground for British representation, he heard of the plans to launch The Monkees with their own weekly TV show. It was obvious that there would be conflict between British born Monkee Davy Jones and British born Davie Jones who sang with The Lower Third. Pitt, even though he was not David's manager at the time, cabled London suggesting that David should change his name. This move shows a tremendous optimism in David's future for at that time neither of the David Joneses had been heard of by anyone.

Davie Jones With The King Bees
Liza Jane (Conn) / **Louie Louie Go Home**
(Revere)
Vocalion Pop V 9221.   Released June 1964.
Musical Director: Leslie Conn.
Producer: Leslie Conn.

The Manish Boys
I Pity The Fool (Malone) / **Take My Tip** (Jones)
Parlophone R 5250.   Released March 5, 1965.
Producer: Shel Talmy.

Davy Jones and The Lower Third
You've Got A Habit Of Leaving (Jones) / **Baby Loves That Way** (Jones)
Parlophone R 5315.   Released August 20, 1965.
Producer: Shel Talmy.

KEN PITT, DAVID'S FIRST MANAGER.

DAVIE JONES AND THE LOWER THIRD. (PHOTO: EMI RECORDS)

David changed his name to David Bowie. He has said that he took the name from the famous American knife but according to Kenneth Pitt it is also a family name somewhere on his mother's side.

By this time Horton had arranged yet another record deal for David, this time with Pye, working with record producer Tony Hatch. On January 14, 1966 Pye released the first David Bowie record, 'Can't Help Thinking About Me'. By this time David was very involved in the Carnaby Street Mod scene and the recording is reminiscent of The Kinks or The Who from this period. The Pye press release which publicised the record described the change of name to Bowie. Headed 'Davie Jones Is Back In His Locker' it quotes David as saying, 'There are too many Davie Joneses. David Jones is my real name and when I first turned professional two years ago and my pirate-like character was just right at the time and the name fitted in with the image I wanted to give myself.'

During the next three months, Kenneth Pitt, Ralph Horton, David and both his parents were engaged in negotiations concerning a management contract with Pitt. This was finally agreed and David signed for a five year period in April 1966. David was still only 19 years old and though he roughed it to a certain extent by sleeping in the back of the van after gigs and suffering the usual problems of a struggling new band, he had a comfortable place at home to go to whenever he wanted, unlike many of the new musicians of the time. The life on the road was getting to the members of The Lower Third and they finally broke up. David was left with a solo career.

Shortly after the release of 'Can't Help Thinking About Me', an interview with David appeared in Melody Maker. The article said that he and Tony Hatch were writing a musical score and numbers for a TV show. It also said that David designed shirts and suits for John Stephen, the then-fashionable Carnaby Street Mod tailor. David also talked about his interest in Tibetan Buddhism apparently not knowing Tibet was closed to visitors.

'I want to go to Tibet. It's a fascinating place y'know? I'd like to take a holiday and have a look inside the monasteries. The Tibetan monks, Lamas, bury themselves inside mountains for weeks and only eat every three days. They're ridiculous — and it's said that they live for centuries.

'As far as I'm concerned the whole idea of western life, that's the life we live now, is wrong. These are hard convictions to put into songs though. At the moment I write nearly all of my songs round London. No, I should say the people who live in London — and the lack of real life they have. The majority just don't know what real life is.

'Several of the younger teenagers' programmes wouldn't play 'Can't Help Thinking About Me' because it is about leaving home. The number relates several incidents in every teenager's life, and leaving home is something which always comes up.

'Tony Hatch and I wanted to do another number I had written. It goes down very well in the stage act and lots of fans said I should have released it — but Tony and I thought the words were a bit strong. It tells the story of life as some teenagers saw it — but we didn't think the lyrics were quite up many people's street. I do it on stage though and we're probably keeping it for an EP or maybe an LP. Hope, hope! It's called 'Now You've Met The London Boys' and mentions pills and generally belittles the London night life scene.

'I've lived in London and been brought up here and I find it's a great subject to write songs about. And remember, with all original numbers the audiences are hearing numbers they've

1966

never heard before so this makes for a varied stage act. It's risky because the kids aren't familiar with the tunes but I'm sure it makes their musical life more interesting.'

But 'London Boys' had to wait until the end of 1966 for release through a different record company and a different producer. Bowie's relationship with Tony Hatch deteriorated and there were reports of arguments. Hatch released two more undistinguished singles, 'Do Anything You Say' and 'I Dig Everything' before calling it a day. The latter was released on August 19th, two days before David began another series of Sunday afternoon appearances at The Marquee. The Sunday afternoon set was to attract foreign students at the height of the tourist season and the place would be crowded with French and German teenagers. David did a solo acoustic set while his mother sat in the front row wearing a straw hat. David's show stopper was 'When You Walk Through A Storm' contrary to his statement that he only performed his own material. In keeping with Pitt's idea of creating an all round entertainer he began to find David work in TV and films. For the next couple of years David appeared in diverse projects, such as a dance sequence on a TV commercial advertising

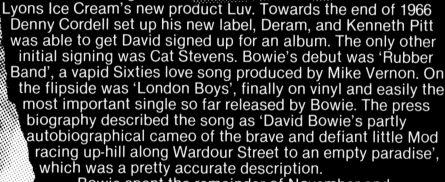

Lyons Ice Cream's new product Luv. Towards the end of 1966 Denny Cordell set up his new label, Deram, and Kenneth Pitt was able to get David signed up for an album. The only other initial signing was Cat Stevens. Bowie's debut was 'Rubber Band', a vapid Sixties love song produced by Mike Vernon. On the flipside was 'London Boys', finally on vinyl and easily the most important single so far released by Bowie. The press biography described the song as 'David Bowie's partly autobiographical cameo of the brave and defiant little Mod racing up-hill along Wardour Street to an empty paradise', which was a pretty accurate description.

Bowie spent the remainder of November and December working on his first album, 'Love You Till Tuesday', which seems to have occupied four sessions in 1966 and a final one in February 1967. Cordell wasn't spending much money on studio time for his new label and Bowie later commented, 'That first album I did in about fifteen minutes. You could say it was rushed!'

15

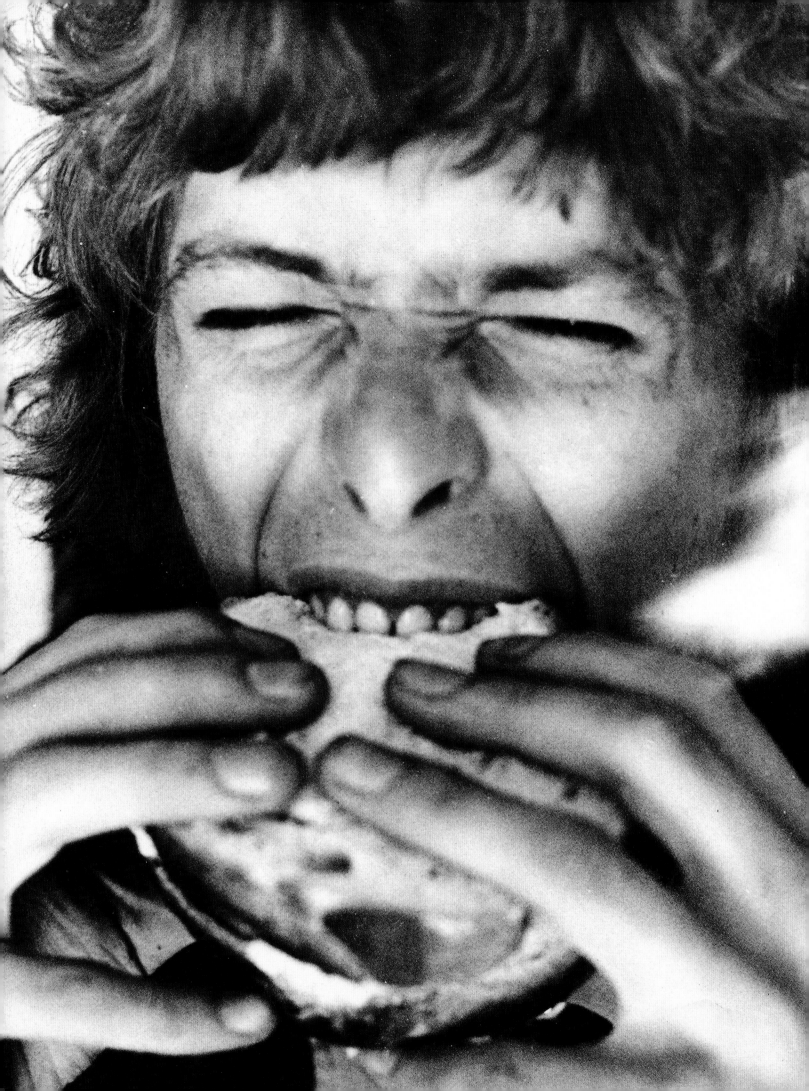

David entered the year of the flower children very quietly. He was living in a spare room in Ken Pitt's flat at 39 Manchester Street, Marylebone, W1 in the West End of London and putting the finishing touches to his first album. He was spending more and more time studying Tibetan Buddhism with Chime yongdon Rinpoche at his centre in Hampstead and visiting the Tibetan monastery of Samye-Ling in Eskdalemuir, Dumfriesshire in Scotland which was run by the master of Vajrayana meditation, Chogyam Trungpa Rinpoche. According to interviews he was also involved with the activities of the Tibet Society in Eccleston Square who were concerned with the welfare of Tibetan refugees.

The other side of the year of the summer of love emerged when he released 'The Laughing Gnome' on April 14. A giggly pot-head sub-Chipmonk song with David playing with the varispeed and set well in the English hippy tradition of Gnome songs (Syd Barrett, Tomorrow, etc ...) To Bowie's horror, this embarrassing record was re-issued by Decca in 1973, when it reached number 4 in the charts and sold a quarter million copies. Typical of Bowie, the record was one of total contrast for on the flipside was 'The Gospel According To Tony Day', a cynical and depressing account of the values and aspirations of a number of mythical friends.

In May David received his advance money for the Deram album and in June, finally, it came out. 'Love You Till Tuesday' was produced by Mike Vernon who described David as 'One of the brightest talents I have ever recorded'. The public, however, were curiously unmoved and the album soon appeared in bargain bins.

The failure of his debut album seems to have had a sobering effect on David and he characteristically changed direction.

'Love You Till Tuesday' was released as a single but still went nowhere. It didn't matter because David already had two new interests: film and mime.

In September David began work on his first film, called 'The Image', a twenty minute short made by writer, director Michael Armstrong for Border Films (London) Limited. The film is silent and only has two characters, The Artist played by Michael Byrne and The Boy played by David. It was filmed on location in a derelict house in which The Artist has a studio. He is painting a portrait of The Boy from a photograph propped up on a nearby table. The Artist seems to be frightened and goes to the window to investigate a noise but there is no-one there. As he returns to the painting David's face appears at the window, nose squashed against the glass, soaked to the skin from the rain. In fact he was hanging on the window sill for life since it was an upstairs window, while buckets of water were poured over him to simulate rain.

The Artist is disturbed and when David miraculously appears behind him in the hallway, The Artist punches him about the face and stomach, then grabs a bronze bust and kills him by banging him on the head with it.

Though The Boy is now supposed to be dead this doesn't turn out to be a satisfactory way of disposing of him as The Boy appears again, standing in the doorway behind The Artist. Then he's outside the window again, then in the doorway and so on. The Artist makes a run for it and hides in the bathroom. David peeps in through the bubbled glass window.

Fortunately for The Artist there is a handy broken knife in the bathroom since, when he turns round, there is The Boy standing looking at him. Bowie has a dramatic scene at this point when, after The Artist had knifed him a few times in the gut, The Boy artistically falls gurgling down a flight of stairs. The Artist, remembering how The Image missed out on dying the last time, takes no chances and stabs The Boy a few more times in the back of the neck for good

1967

luck. This seems to do the trick. It is now The Artist's turn for a major scene. Filled with remorse he tears the paper from the easel and falls weeping on it, ripping and tearing at it as he hits the floor. The film ends. It was not a box office success though it did show up sandwiched between two sex movies in a Soho porn house in 1973.

David earned £30 from this venture which even Pitt described as 'a quite dreadful film'. A chance meeting took him in another entirely different direction.

David attended a one man mime show given by Lindsay Kemp at a small Covent Garden theatre. During the intermission he strolled outside for a cigarette but paused when he heard his own album being played as the interval music. Encouraged and flattered, he went to the stage door after the show and introduced himself to Kemp. Lindsay Kemp was an internationally known mime who had studied and worked with Marcel Marceau (says Kemp, 'I talk about studying with him and I don't tell anybody I only had three lessons'). He had worked with The Ballet Rambert, the Commedia Dell Arte, the Kulouki, Marceau and in films with everyone from Fellini to Ken Russell. He was a mime, a painter, and actor and a teacher and it was understandable that David would be attracted to him. David once described their relationship:

'I gained an extraordinary amount from being with him. Lindsay introduced me to things like Cocteau and The Theatre of the Absurd, Antonin Artaud and the whole idea of restructuring and going against what people generally expect — sometimes for shock value and sometimes as an educational force but whatever. He just gave me the idea that you can experiment with the arts and do things and take dangerous risks that you wouldn't do in real life so you can use it as an experimental area for trying out new life styles without actually having to take the consequences.'

David and Lindsay came to an agreement that David would write material for Lindsay's shows in exchange for free mime lessons. Eventually David became an active part of the Lindsay Kemp Troupe but initially he just attended Kemp's classes at The Dance Centre in Floral Street, Covent Garden. David talked more about Lindsay in an interview with Richard Cromelin:

'Lindsay Kemp was a living Pierrot. He lived and talked Pierrot. He was tragic and dramatic and everything in his life was theatrical. And so the stage thing for him was just an extension of himself. There's a lot of material from his private life that would beat any script. But we utilized the figures of Columbine, Pierrot and Scaramouche, what have you — traditional figures. We used some Genet, Lindsay was very fond of Genet, and we used some Oscar Wilde, some Joyce.'

David's first appearance as a mime was with Lindsay Kemp in 'Pierrot In Turquoise' at the Oxford New Theatre on December 28, 1967. But David had not given up his musical career. On November 10th he appeared on the Dutch TV show, 'Fan Club' and on December 18th he was on BBC's 'Top Gear'.

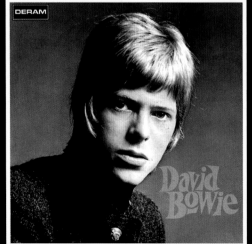

' **Love You Till Tuesday** '
Deram DML 1007.   Released June 1967.
Producer: Mike Vernon.
Arranger: Dek Fearnley, David Bowie.
1.   **Uncle Arthur** (Bowie)
2.   **Sell Me A Coat** (Bowie)
3.   **Rubber Band** (Bowie)
4.   **Love You Till Tuesday** (Bowie)
5.   **There Is A Happy Land** (Bowie)
6.   **We are Hungry Men** (Bowie)
7.   **When I Live My Dreams** (Bowie)
8.   **Little Bombardier** (Bowie)
9.   **Silly Boy Blue** (Bowie)
10.   **Come And Buy My Toys** (Bowie)
11.   **Join The Gang** (Bowie)
12.   **She's Got Medals** (Bowie)
13.   **Maid Of Bond Street** (Bowie)
14.   **Please Mr. Gravedigger** (Bowie)
Tracks 4 and 7 have later, non-sequential matrix numbers.
Re-issued as 'The World Of David Bowie' with some track changes. See later listing.

The Laughing Gnome (Bowie) / **The Gospel According To Tony Day** (Bowie)
Deram DM 123.   Released April 14, 1967.
Re-issued September 8, 1973.
Producer: Mike Vernon.

Love You Till Tuesday (Bowie) / **Did You Ever Have A Dream** (Bowie)
Deram DM 135.   Released July 15, 1967.
Producer: Mike Vernon.
Musical Director: Side A, Ivor Raymonde; Side B, Dek Fearnley.
Side B originally intended for release on the 'Love You Till Tuesday' album. Side A was the title track.

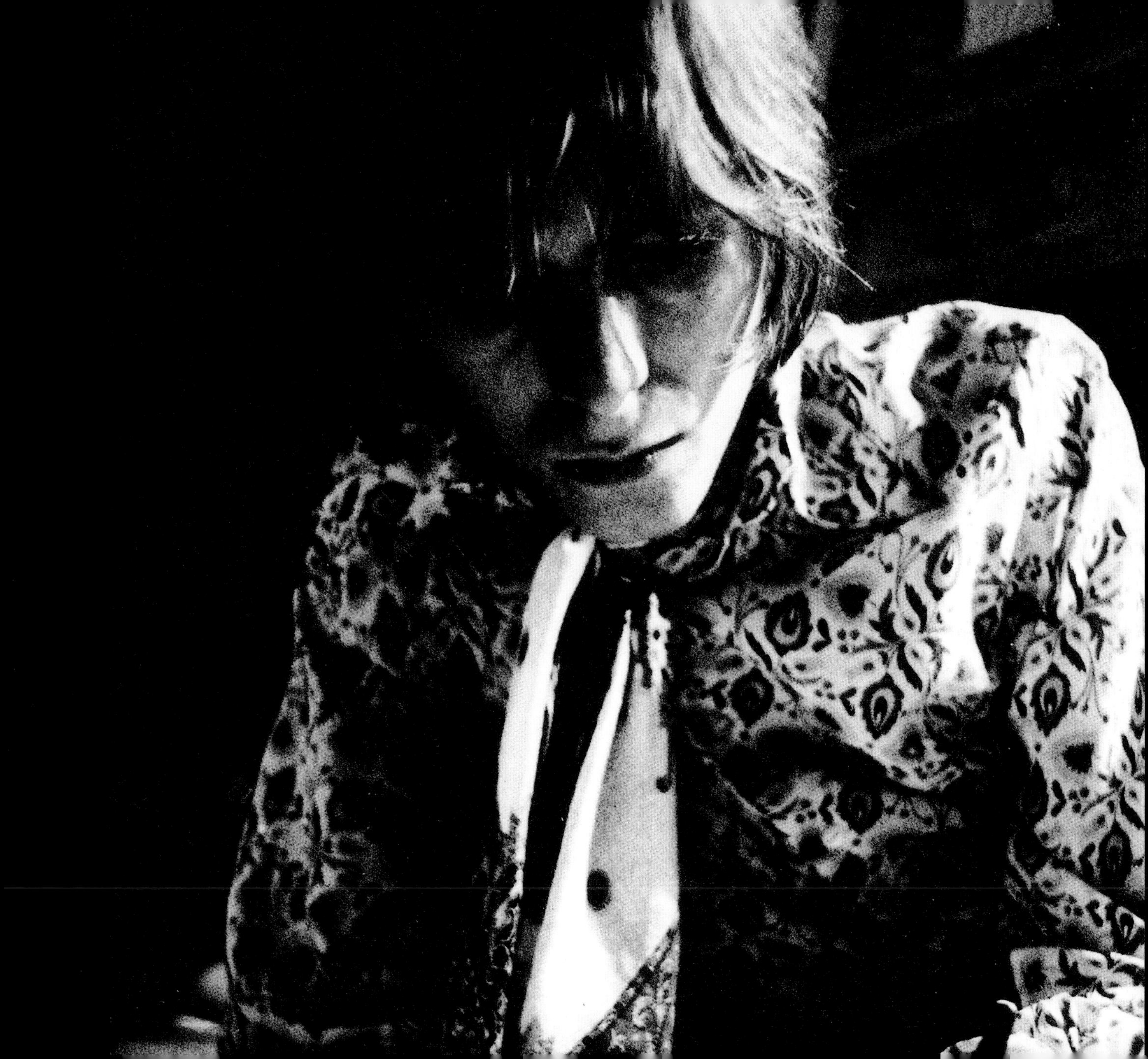

David followed up the December mime performance by doing three dates at Rose Hill in Cumberland with The Lindsay Kemp Troupe on January 3, 4 and 5th, for which he was paid £40.

Then David fell in love. The girl was Hermione Farthingale who came from Sevenoaks in Kent where her father was a solicitor. She was a quiet attractive girl with red hair. David first met her while attending Lindsay Kemp's classes at the Floral Street Dance Centre but it wasn't until January 30, 1968 that they first got together. They were booked to dance a minuet together in a BBC2 TV costume drama 'The Pistol Shot' in which they appeared dressed in powdered wigs and full 18th century costume.

It was not long before they decided to live together and they found a very small flat in a converted Victorian villa on Gunter Grove, SW10 which had an overgrown garden in front. David and Hermione lived together for almost a year.

In March 1968, David did more work with the Lindsay Kemp Troupe. From March 5 until the 16th he performed in 'Pierrot In Turquoise' at the Mercury Theatre, Notting Hill Gate, London. This was followed by performances from March 25th until the 30th at the Little Theatre, Palmers Green. This, apart from a TV show in 1970, was the total amount of work done by David with Kemp contrary to the stories that he spent two years working with the Lindsay Kemp Troupe.

David tried to use his experience with Kemp to create a mime of his own and on June 3rd, as the support act for Marc Bolan, he presented a 20 minute play in mime and song at the Royal Festival Hall, London. The piece concerned the plight of a young religious boy living in Tibet after the Chinese takeover. The concert was a disaster because the audience had no idea what was supposed to be going on.

He decided to form a small mime troupe of his own. Called Feathers, it consisted of himself, Hermione and bass player John Hutchinson, 'Hutch', who had been in one of his many backing groups. They performed at The Arts Lab in Drury Lane, Covent Garden, run by Jim Haynes and Jack Henry Moore. The Arts Lab featured experimental music, drama and films, specialising in underground films and there was also an art gallery, a restaurant and a book stall. Jim lived in the back. Most of the groups who performed there did so for the exposure and just passed the hat round afterwards. Feathers never made much impact but the Arts Lab impressed David so much that, in 1969, when Arts Labs were popping up all across the country, David decided to start one of his own.

Feathers played The Country Club, Hampstead, on November 17th. They played The Arts Lab on December 6th and the next day were at Sussex University in Brighton, but things turned sour with Hermione and she left David and Feathers. David tried one more appearance alone with John Hutchinson at the University of Surrey on February 11, 1969 but that was their final performance. Hutch later gave up music and went back to his home town of Hull with his wife and family to work as a draughtsman.

Feathers was, however, preserved on film. Ken Pitt had been so struck by David's song 'Love You Till Tuesday' that he decided to use it as the title of a film of David's songs that could be sold as a TV special. He invested £7,000 in the project but it was far too avant garde for the TV companies with Feathers mime show and strange camera angles and fast shifting images. When TV companies did need some footage of David it was already out of date because 'Love You Till Tuesday' was when he was in his Anthony Newley phase and in fact the title track is

1968

so like Anthony Newley as to be indistinguishable. One very good thing did come out of the movie, however.

The film was to consist mainly of material from the 'Love You Till Tuesday' album, but Pitt thought that some original material was also needed. David went off to write some songs. He went to see a movie, Stanley Kubrick's '2001: A Space Odyssey'. Inspired, David went home and wrote 'Space Oddity', parodying the name of the movie.

Pitt immediately recognised its potential and they filmed it a few days later with David in a silver space suit crawling about in a space capsule — the film which was used on TV much later to promote the record. At this time, however, the film was inserted with the other Feathers scenes in 'Love You Till Tuesday'. The film was made just after David wrote the song, sometime around September-October 1968, but it was to be another nine months before the record was released.

In the meantime David had other things to do. When he and Hermione broke up he gave up their little flat and moved back to Ken Pitt's spare room in Marylebone. It was the beginning of 1969 and a time when the Arts Lab movement was burgeoning. There were Labs in Wales, Manchester, Brighton, Swindon, even Cheltenham David felt moved to open one himself in suburban Beckenham near his parents' place in Bromley.

THE ONLY PICTURES EVER TAKEN OF DAVID DOING MIME: HE IS STANDING ON KEN PITT'S COFFEE TABLE.

23

The Beckenham Arts Lab, despite its rather grand name, was in reality a spare room in The Three Tuns pub in the High Street, started by David 'to promote the ideals and creative processes of the underground'. David was fully involved with the London underground scene at this point and, even with his growing recording and performing commitments, he devoted an enormous amount of time and energy and money to the project. Most interviews he did at the time talked about nothing else. He described the Lab in detail in an interview with Mary Finnegan published in the International Times, the underground newspaper of the day and main source of news of Arts Lab activity. The interview was conducted just after 'Space Oddity' had been released and Mary, who worked with him on the Beckenham Arts Lab, asked him if he would live within the same social framework if the record went to number one:

'Yes, why not? We'll invite the straight journalists back to your flat after the folk club and Bowie will still be doing the same things and still not answering the same questions. The people who are attracted by the charts will see an Arts Lab actually happening because my relationship with my own scene won't change.

'Part of my motivation in doing a hit parade number is to promote the arts labs along with it, but without elitist attitudes. Arts Labs should be for everyone not just the so-called turned-on minority. We need energy from all directions, heads and skin-heads alike.

'Here we are in Beckenham with a group of people creating their own momentum without the slightest concern for attitudes, tradition or pre-ordained moralities. It's alive, healthy and new and it matters to me more than anything else.'

Breaking up with Hermione had hurt David very deeply. He was obviously very much in love with her and the wound caused by her leaving may never have healed. Even six years later he was describing love as 'disgusting' and insisting that he didn't love his wife, Angie. He wrote a sad ballad of love lost, 'Letter To Hermione' which appeared on his next album. It is the kind of song he has never written since.

In February he resurrected his one man mime show about the trials and tribulations of a young religious boy in Communist Tibet and took it out on the road as a support act for Marc Bolan's Tyrannosaurus Rex tour. They played The Free Trade Hall, Manchester on February 22; Colston Hall, Bristol on February 23rd; Liverpool Philharmonic on March 1st and The Brighton Dome on March 8th. And then came 'Space Oddity'.

It was at this time that David met someone who was to have a big impact on his career and direction. A young American girl, fresh out of a Swiss finishing school, was on a visit to England hoping to somehow get into the record business. Mary Angela Barnett met David at a press reception at The Speakeasy to launch King Crimson. David described how they got together in an interview with Playboy Magazine:

'Angela and I knew each other because we were both going out with the same man. Another one of her boyfriends, a talent scout for Mercury Records, took her to a show at The Roundhouse, where I happened to be playing. He hated me. She thought I was great. Ultimately she threatened to leave him if he didn't sign me. So he signed me. I married Angela and we both continued to see the mutual boyfriend.'

Angie was a perfect companion for David. She was widely travelled, spoke four languages and introduced him to a whole range of new ideas and interests. They began to see a lot of each other. They travelled, using a car David borrowed from his father, and she became, in effect, his road manager.

25

1969

Then came 'Space Oddity'. Phillips, on the strength of the demo cut for the movie 'Love You Till Tuesday', were convinced that it would be a hit. David was fortunate in that when he came to record it again, the record was arranged by Paul Buckmaster and produced by Gus Dudgeon, both of whom have gone on to great fame and fortune with their association with Elton John. At this point in time, Dudgeon was so new to the game that he hadn't heard that producers can claim royalties on records and, since record companies don't give money away, he received nothing when the record hit the charts. 'Space Oddity' was recorded on June 20, 1969 at Trident Studios, the same day that David signed with Mercury Records.

David was also fortunate in the release of the song coinciding with the American moon landing. The timing was perfect and the flight of Apollo certainly gave the record a lot of topical airplay. The BBC even used it as a theme to their film of the landing — a strange choice if they had ever seriously examined the lyrics of the song. But it wasn't mere topicality that sold the record. It's a remarkable piece of storytelling and in the space of a few minutes Bowie creates a mood and tells a complex story, using the wonderfully simple device of Major Tom's communications with Ground Control.

The International Times interview asked David if he saw Major Tom as an alter-ego figure: 'Well, we drew this parallel that the publicity image of a spaceman at work is an automaton rather than a human being and my Major Tom is nothing if not a human being. It comes from a feeling of sadness about this aspect of the space thing. It has been dehumanised so I wrote a song-farce about it to try and relate science and human emotion. I suppose it's an antidote to space fever really.'

He explained it as an attempt to express the totality of all things, a common sixties underground preoccupation. 'At the end of the song, Major Tom is completely emotionless and expresses no view at all about where he's at. He gives up thinking completely ... he's fragmenting. At the end of the song his mind is completely blown. He's everything then.'

With 'Space Oddity' in the charts David took off with Kenneth Pitt to represent Britain at the Malta Song Festival. Pitt was still pushing the Tommy Steele all-round entertainer and David was up for the travel. They stayed at the Hilton Hotel and David exchanged his hippy gear for a suit that had been made for the movie. He sang 'When I Live My Dream' to a backing orchestra made up of musicians from the British Army, The United States Navy and the Spanish embassy. There were fifteen countries competing but David won easily and received a little statuette.

The festival was 'paired' with one in Italy and so the fifteen contestants then flew off to the Italian Song Festival. This time there were no backing musicians and the best the organisers could come up with at short notice was three Italian accordionists who couldn't read music. Fortunately David had with him a backing tape from the album track and was able to use that. He arrived back in London in the best of spirits carrying a statuette with the Virgin Mary on top of it.

He arrived to find his father in hospital and only semi-conscious. David ran round to the hospital, still clutching the statuette. His father managed a smile when David held it up but Haywood Stenton Jones died that night of lobar pneumonia. The date was August 5, 1969. David had always been very close to his father and was totally shattered.

David handled his father's estate. His brother Terry was unable to help since he was in a mental institution and had been ever since David was in his early teens. David closed up the

Space Oddity (Bowie) / **Wild Eyed Boy From Freecloud** (Bowie)
Philips BF 1801. Released July 11, 1969.
Producer: Gus Dudgeon.
Arrangers: Paul Buckmaster, David Bowie.

house in Bromley and his mother went to live in a flat. He saw less and less of her, eventually not contacting her at all.

David threw himself into work: Phillips released the 'David Bowie' album and David put his energy into the Arts Lab and, after a few months felt strong enough to go out on the road.

His father's death made him retreat more into his small circle of close friends for support. At that time they were Marc Bolan, his wife June, Angie, and Tony Visconti. Manager Ken Pitt was left on the outside. Pitt was from another generation and didn't fit in with the approach to life of Bolan and Visconti who both frowned on the idea of managers anyway. David was very influenced by Marc and Marc's opinion and approval became all important to him.

In a classic piece of mis-timing Pitt sent David out on the road the month before his album was released. Manager Andrew Loog Oldham had put together a new band, Humble Pie, based around Peter Frampton and Steve Marriott. Oldham hired David to put on a fifteen minute mime act and was horrified when David walked on stage and did a solo acoustic set with a Gibson 12 string. David had finished with his mime period.

It was the first time that David and Frampton had shared a stage since their old school show. Frampton, though much younger, was already an old pro compared to the sheltered life David had been living. Going out on the road was a rude awakening for David. He had been doing quite well financially with one-off gigs on the strength of his chart success but this was a proper tour. He received only £400 for the whole thing and it was rather less than an artistic success as he later described:

'It was very hard. I was on in front of these gum-chewing skin-heads. As soon as I appeared, looking a bit like Bob Dylan with this curly hair and denims, I was whistled and booed. At one point I even had cigarettes thrown at me. Isn't that awful? It turned me off the business. I was totally paranoid.'

But it wasn't the tour that surprised him as much as the different things that happen with the audiences. He was used to the silent, respectful atmosphere of folk clubs and his own Arts Lab and when he went out on the road from October 8th till the 26th with the Humble Pie tour there was no way that he was prepared for what happened.

'It was my first tour and I never stopped being surprised that the concerts even went on. It appeared to be badly organised to me but I suppose everybody knew what they were doing. For me it was nothing near an artistic success. I throw myself on the mercy of the audience and I really need them to respond to me. But all the same, I'm determined to be an entertainer — clubs, cabaret, concerts, the lot. There is too much false pride within the pop scene, groups and singers decrying cabaret without ever having seen the inside of a northern night club.'

But if the skinheads didn't like him, the girls certainly did. At Perth screaming young girls rushed the stage when he sang 'Wild Eyed Young Boy From Freecloud'. The amazed Bowie described it in an interview:

'I stand bemused by it all, especially this teenybop thing. I would never have believed in a million years that people would scream at me. I am really incredulous. Now I'm receiving the most extraordinary stuff through the post, crucifixes, gonky things with big eyes, fluffy toys and funny little letters that are sometimes weird with girls promising to do very strange things to me...'

By November David and Angela had found themselves a place to live. It was an enormous apartment in Haddon Hall, Beckenham, near to the Arts Lab. Haddon Hall was a sprawling

27

Victorian thirty roomed folly originally built for an industrialist and once occupied by a Sainsbury. It was complete with a ballroom and turrets with weather vanes. The building was divided into flats and David's real address was Flat 7, 42 Southend Road, Beckenham, Kent, not Haddon Hall as he rather pompously headed all his letters. His friend Tony Visconti was so impressed with the place that he moved down there as well and had a flat there until he married singer Mary Hopkin by which time David was long gone.

On November 14, Phillips released the album 'David Bowie', complete with curly-locked David peering through an Op-Art construction by Vaserelli and a psychedelic|back cover. The album was produced by Tony Visconti at Trident Studios in Soho. David later described it as 'great drooling nine minute epics' but the album caught the spirit of the sixties. He did his obligatory Bob Dylan imitation on 'Unwashed and Somewhat Slightly Dazed' and a fullblown freakout version of 'Memory of a Free Festival' which draws its inspiration from everyone from the Grateful Dead to The Beatles. The number had an anthem-like, haunting quality, already nostalgic for the sixties though 1969 was not quite over. Next to 'Space Oddity' in its full 5½ minute glory, 'Free Festival' was the most popular song on the album.

It was based on a festival organised by Bowie and company at the Beckenham Arts Lab: 'It was a very unusual kind of festival because it was all local people. No big names or anything, the idea was just to use people from the area who never got a chance to be seen by more than a hundred people because they only do tiny clubs and this day they were playing to over five thousand people, which was great! And they went down very well. Maybe the quality was kind of dodgy but the enthusiasm was tremendous.'

The album was promoted with 'An Evening With David Bowie' held at The Purcell Room, on the South Bank in London on November 20th. David was backed by a local Beckenham band called Copus and the audience was packed with his friends and people from Phillips Records. David was on top form and the concert was a great success and was regarded by many people as the best thing he had ever done. To his great distress there were no press there. As part of his growing rift from Kenneth Pitt, David had hired the hall himself and had neglected to invite any critics. He was furious at himself and retired hurt to Haddon Hall.

The album, strangely, received hardly any critical attention. Maybe the critics were too busy listening to the sounds coming over from the States, it's hard to understand since he had just had a hit single. With the critics overlooking it it followed that the record buyers ignored it also. David was astounded. He had not expected a chart position but had expected the album to establish his musical reputation. He withdrew into the security of Angie, Tony Visconti and Marc Bolan, spending almost all of his time with them. 'I was in the depths of despair. I became disillusioned. I used to have periods, weeks on end, when I just couldn't cope any more. I'd slump into myself. I felt so depressed. I really felt so aimless — and this torrential feeling of 'What's it all for anyway?'

The only light relief at the end of the sixties came when he was presented to Princess Margaret after a 'Save Rave '69' charity show at the London Palladium on November 30th, in aid of the Invalid Children's Aid Association. He appeared alongside Dusty Springfield, The Equals, The Mojos, Marmalade, The Settlers and Tiny Tim.

Angela had to go to Cyprus to see her parents who were based there. There was a postal strike on and so all of David's letters were held up. They all arrived at once on Christmas. One of them said, 'This year we will marry'. Angela was astonished. She later told The Chicago

(PHOTO: AL JOHNSON)

'David Bowie'
Philips SBL 7912.   Released November 4, 1969.
Producers: Track 1: Gus Dudgeon.   Tracks 2-9: Tony Visconti.
Arrangers: Track 1: Paul Buckmaster, David Bowie.   Tracks 2-9: Tony Visconti, David Bowie.
Studio: Trident, London.
Engineers: Ken Scott, Malcolm Toft and Barry Sheffield.

1. **Space Oddity** (Bowie)
2. **Unwashed And Somewhat Slightly Dazed** (Bowie)
3. **Letter To Hermione** (Bowie)
4. **Cygnet Committee** (Bowie)
5. **Janine** (Bowie)
6. **An Occasional Dream** (Bowie)
7. **Wild Eyed Boy From Freecloud** (Bowie)
8. **God Knows I'm Good** (Bowie)
9. **Memory Of A Free Festival** (Bowie)

David Bowie: Vocals, 12-string guitar, stylophone, kalimba, Rosedale electric chord organ.

Keith Christmas: Guitar.
Mick Wayne: Guitar.
Tim Renwick: Guitar, flutes and recorders.
Honk: Bass.
Tony Visconti: Bass, flutes and recorders.
Herbie Flowers: Bass.
John Cambridge: Drums.
Terry Cox: Drums.
Rick Wakeman: Mellotron, electric harp-sichord.
Paul Buckmaster: Cello.
Benny Marshall: Harmonica.
Track 7 is a different version from the B side of the single 'Space Oddity'.
The album was re-issued by RCA under the title of 'Space Oddity' as RCA LSP 4813 in November 1972.

(PHOTO: AL JOHNSON)

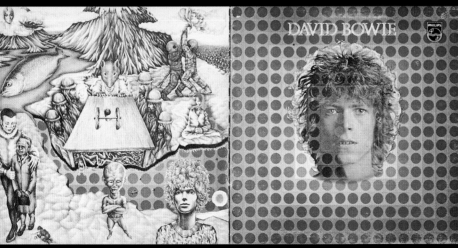

Sunday Mirror: 'I was quite shocked when I read it. It was so romantic and unlike him. He phoned me the next day and I told him I was coming back. He met me. We never actually discussed the idea of getting married again; he just went ahead and made the arrangements and we were wed... in the spring. I suppose if I hadn't married David I'd now be a fat Greek type lady with a large family in Cyprus.'

David's growing cult following was gradually undermining the Arts Lab because more and more people were regarding it just as 'David's Club' and would arrive, watch David's folk set and then leave before anyone else came on. But David remained involved and enthusiastic, devoting more time in interviews to describing it than in promoting his own career. One such interview was particularly candid about hippies and was critical about the original Drury Lane Arts Lab where he first played with The Flowers. The interview was with Chris Welch in September 1969:

'I run an arts lab which is my chief occupation. It's in Beckenham and I think it's the best in the country. There isn't one pseud involved. All the people are real — like labourers or bank clerks. It started out as a folk club. Arts labs generally have such a bad reputation as pseud places. 'There's a lot of talent in the green belt and there is a load of tripe in Drury Lane. I think the Arts Lab movement is extremely important and should take over from the youth club concept as a social service.

'The people who come are completely pacifist and we get a lot of co-operation from the police in our area. They are more than helpful. Respect breeds respect. We've got a few greasers who come and a few skinheads who are just as enthusiastic.

'I think a lot of skinheads are better than hippies and the hippie cult is so obviously middle class and snobbish which is why the skinheads don't like them.

'The hippies don't know about people, they really don't. They don't know what it's like to see three heavies go after their sister and all the other things that happen in a skinhead's environment.

'Nobody wants the skinheads — the schools don't want them or the youth clubs and the arts labs don't want to know them least of all.

'When UFO started they would never let the Mods in and now they are getting their own back and getting more violent.

'We started our lab a few months ago with poets and artists who just came along. It's got bigger and bigger and now we have our own light show and sculptures, etcetera. And I never knew there were so many sitar players in Beckenham.'

David's commitment to the arts lab didn't stop him from playing gigs. He opened the new decade with a concert at Johnston Hall, Aberdeen University, on January 30th, was at the Marquee on February 3rd, sharing the bill with Junior's Eyes and appeared on Grampian TV's 'Cairngorm Ski Night' on February 27th. But the next day David revealed his new lineup:

Billed as 'Hype, David Bowie's new electric band', they supported High Tide at the Basildon Arts Centre on February 28th. Hype consisted of producer Tony Visconti on bass, John Cambridge on drums (he was on the Phillips 'David Bowie' album) and Mick Ronson on guitar. Visconti had met Ronson during the sessions for Michael Chapman's 'Fully Qualified Survivor' album and introduced him to David since he knew David was looking for a guitarist and thought they would get along.

He was right. Ronson moved into David's Beckenham home and they spent weeks rehearsing in the basement and planning their future strategy. 'David just knew he'd be famous one day' recalls Ronson.

On March 6th, Phillips released 'The Prettiest Star', arranged and produced by Visconti, however Ronson did not play on this version. Marc Bolan took the lead guitar and when it was re-recorded for the 'Aladdin Sane' album, Ronson followed Bolan's line very faithfully. Visconti played bass.

Also in March Decca decided to re-issue the 'Love You Till Tuesday' album in their 'World Of' series. They dropped two tracks and substituted instead the four remaining tracks in their vaults including the single 'London Boys'.

Angie's visa was about to expire and, since she could remain in Britain as Mrs David Bowie, she and David got married. The marriage took place at Bromley Register Office on March 20th. David explained his other reasons for marrying in the 1976 Playboy interview:

'I realized that she'd be one of the very few women I'd be capable of living with for more than a week. She is remarkably pleasant to keep coming back to. And, for me, she always will be. There's nobody more demanding than me. Not physically, necessarily, but mentally. I'm very strenuous. Very intense about anything I do. I scare away most people I've lived with.'

In an interview with George Tremlett David said that it was Angie's visa problem which prompted their marriage. 'If it hadn't been for that we probably wouldn't have got married. To us the legal ceremonies of marriage are just a formality that don't mean very much if a couple cease to be in love with each other afterwards. Although we were in love with each other, we didn't feel the need to get married to prove it. The actual ceremony didn't mean that much to us.'

For this reason, David and Angie tried to keep the marriage as quiet as possible, not telling Angie's parents, who lived in Cyprus and probably wouldn't have been able to attend anyway, and not telling David's mother, who in any case disliked Angie intensely. Kenneth Pitt did not get invited either.

Somehow David's mother found out and was waiting on the steps outside the register office when they arrived. But even with her there there were only six people present. 'We wanted a very quiet wedding with hardly anyone there but ourselves' said David. Afterwards they all went back to Haddon Hall and watched television because it was raining.

It was an uneasy period for David. He was experimenting more and more with gender roles. Using his experience as a Carnaby Street designer he began designing unisex clothing and even men's dresses for himself and was all the time working on 'The Man Who Sold The

1970

World'. A transitional album in which he wrapped up all the loose ends before making the big jump which would bring him stardom. It's an album which analyses his childhood: 'The Width Of The Circle' and even his family. He has said in various interviews that 'All The Madmen' is about his brother Terry.

On June 26th, Phillips released a new version of the popular 'Memory Of A Free Festival' from the 'David Bowie' album. It was David's first record in years to use a rock line-up and it marks the beginning of a new era for him. Tony Visconti played bass, Mick Ronson on guitar and Mick Woodmansey on drums, The Spiders From Mars had arrived only no-one knew it yet. They still played under the name of Hype.

1970 was not a great year for David and Angie financially. The latter half was spent working on a new album, 'The Man Who Sold The World' which was a make or break effort on David's part. Angie described the period in an interview: "The Man Who Sold The World' was conceived during a period when we were really having a rough time. We were really poor, we didn't have any money. Our band were really frightened.'

By now the arts lab had closed. Everyone would troop out after David finished playing and the audiences were contributing nothing. 'They wanted some kind of leader at that particular time and I wasn't prepared to be one' David explained.

In an interview coinciding with the release of 'The Man Who Fell To Earth', David told the Melody Maker how his song writing was doing, beginning with his two year old hit, 'Space Oddity':

'I was in the depths of despair then. It was nearly two years ago but I don't forget it because it was an important period and I'm still living off it! It helped me to be accepted as a songwriter and now I've had songs accepted by Three Dog Night and even Gene Vincent. Mickie Most heard a song I wrote and even though I really wanted Leon Russell to sing it I suppose Herman has done it quite well. It's called 'Oh, You Pretty Things'. I don't know if Peter Noone knows what it means, it's all about Homo Superior. Herman goes heavy. He's going to be a slightly more adult entertainer.'

RAK released Peter Noone's version of 'Oh, You Pretty Things' on April 30th.

David dismissed the English album sleeve as 'purely decorative. It's just theatre. I don't know. England is tolerant ...'

Things were changing fast. Largely because David had a new manager in the shape of Tony De Fries who was to make David into a superstar. David originally just wanted De Fries to handle his financial affairs but this was not to be. De Fries had enormous ambition. He saw David as the most famous rock singer in the World and set about manufacturing an image and a programme of world domination.

Tony De Fries first appeared in 1970 when David consulted him about his increasingly tangled financial affairs. Bowie described their first meeting in an interview with Michael Watts: 'He said 'I can get you out of that' and I just sat there and openly wept. I was so relieved that somebody was so strong about things.

'I was always stronger than everybody else around me, more determined and wanting to do more things and everybody else was mousy and didn't want to take any risks. It was like going up a hill trying to drag kids with you, 'Oh come on will you!' — and nobody would go with you. And there was this pillar of strength. It was like everything was going to be different.'

And it was.

The Prettiest Star (Bowie) / Conversation Piece (Bowie)
Mercury MF 1135.   Released March 6, 1970.
Producer: Tony Visconti.
Arranger: Tony Visconti.

'The World of David Bowie'
Decca SPA 58.   Released March 1970.
Producers: Tracks 1-12, 14: Mike Vernon. Track 13: Tony Visconti.
Arrangers: Tracks 1, 3-12, 14: Dek Fearnley. Track 2: Ivor Raymonde. Track 13: Tony Visconti.
1. Uncle Arthur (Bowie)
2. Love You Till Tuesday (Bowie)
3. There Is A Happy Land (Bowie)
4. Little Bombardier (Bowie)
5. Sell Me A Coat (Bowie)
6. Silly Boy Blue (Bowie)
7. The London Boys (Bowie)
8. Karma Man (Bowie)
9. Rubber Man (Bowie)
10. Let Me Sleep Beside You (Bowie)
11. Come And Buy My Toys (Bowie)
12. She's Got Medals (Bowie)
13. In The Heat Of The Morning. (Bowie)
14. When I Live On My Dream (Bowie)
A re-issue of 'Love You Till Tuesday' with some track changes: 'Join The Gang' and 'Please Mr. Gravedigger' have been omitted. The single 'London Boys' plus 'Let Me Sleep Beside You', 'Karma Man' and 'In The Heat Of The Morning' have been added.
The album was re-issued in 1973 with a new sleeve.

Memory Of A Free Festival Part 1 (Bowie) / Memory Of A Free Festival Part 2 (Bowie)
Mercury 6052026.   Released June 26, 1970.
Producer: Tony Visconti.

David was in fact signed to Mercury Records of Chicago, not to Phillips in England a
bosses decided to release the new album first in the USA. The US sleeve was a carto
strange looking gunslinger unlike the famous British 'dress' cover. 'The Man Who Sol
World' sat there in US record racks, not moving an inch except to a few cult fans and
few minutes of airplay on the progressive FM stations, particularly the New York ones
WNEW-FM. Ron Oberman, head of publicity at the Chicago HQ decided that what wa
was a promotional tour of the States so that David could meet the journalists, DJs an
programme directors in New York, Philadelphia, Washington, Chicago, Los Angeles a
Francisco. They didn't have to ask him twice.

David loved New York. The weather was below zero but he soon left the Midtown H
and went browsing at King Karol's giant record store on 42nd Street. Always a self-im
took in the Metropolitan Museum of Art, bought antiques and fell in love with Manhat
Dressed in French beret, flowing long blonde hair and cuffed boots he strolled throug
An old lady stopped him at Broadway and 57th Street to enquire which animal was us
make his woolly greatcoat. 'Teddy bear' replied David.

He set Los Angeles afire by appearing at a reception in a floral patterned gown. He
Mendelsohn from Rolling Stone that the magazine's readers 'can make up their mind
when I begin getting adverse publicity; when I'm found in bed with Raquel Welch's hu
was run in the magazine under a picture of David in a frumpy dress holding a very lim
Fortunately David was back in England before the furore hit. David had had enough tr
with his dresses in the States already. He told Melody Maker, 'I went to America a fev
ago to promote the album and as I knew I was going to Texas I wore a dress. One guy
out a gun and called me a fag. But I thought the dress was beautiful.

Back in England Phillips released 'Holy Holy' and 'Black Country Rock' as a single
January. Two sides which were so influenced by Marc Bolan as to verge on parody. 'E
Country Rock' has such a good imitation of Bolan quavery voice that many critics tho
was him.

It was followed by 'The Man Who Sold The World' in April. The UK division of Merc
Phillips, decided to cash in on the controversy and instead of Mick Weller's cartoon c
the album had in the States, they released it in Britain with a picture of David reclinin
settee in a full length gown. The reaction of English critics was predictable. They lapp
out at the same time felt threatened.

Despite all the interest, 1971 turned out to be a very quiet year for David. He discov
band that he was going to write for and produce: Arnold Corns with Rudy Valentino. A
Corns were originally a group of students at Dulwich College who had been playing f
time under the name Runk. David showed up and introduced a new lead singer, a 19 y
dress designer called Freddie Burrett that David had met in some club or other. Fredc
became Rudy Valentino and wore eye shadow and tight black trousers. 'The Rolling S
finished' proclaimed David, 'Rudy will be the new Mick Jagger'. 'I'm just a dress desig
murmured Rudy. Rudy was also worried about touring. 'I don't want to go anywhere r
they put us on at some of those places out of London I'd get sent up something rotte
those butch provincial blokes.' Rudy needn't have worried, though in April 1971 the pr
record did emerge: 'Moonage Daydream' coupled with 'Hang Onto Yourself' on the B
written and produced by David.

1971

'The Man Who Sold The World'
Mercury 6338041.   Released April 1971.
Producer: Tony Visconti.
Studios: Trident Studios, Advision, London.
1. **The Width Of A Circle** (Bowie)
2. **All The Madmen** (Bowie)
3. **Black Country Rock** (Bowie)
4. **After All** (Bowie)
5. **Running Gun Blues** (Bowie)
6. **Saviour Machine** Bowie)
7. **She Shook Me Cold** (Bowie)
8. **The Man Who Sold The World** (Bowie)
9. **The Supermen** (Bowie)
David Bowie: Guitar, vocals.
Tony Visconti: Electric bass, piano, guitar.
Mick Ronson: Guitar.
Mick Woodmansey: Drums.
Ralph Mace: Moog Synthesizer.
Re-issued by RCA as LSP 4816 in November
1972 with a new sleeve.

Holy Holy (Bowie) / **Black Country Rock**
(Bowie)
Mercury 6052049.   Released January 17,
1971.
Producers: Side A, a Blue Mink Production.
Side B. Tony Visconti.

Meanwhile Tony De Fries was plotting. He had dumped the Mercury/Phillips label and was setting up a deal with RCA. RCA'S A&R man Dennis Katz heard four cuts from the demo tape of 'Hunky Dory' material before deciding that he had to sign.

David kept a fairly low profile. He appeared at the Glastonbury Fayre on June 20, an out-and-out hippy event held under a stage shaped like a huge pyramid and even donated a tape to the triple album that was later released to pay for the free festival: 'Revelations — A Musical Anthology For Glastonbury Fayre', though his own live set does not appear on the album.

Also in June, David showed up at the Paris studios: with him were Geoffrey Alexander, a neighbour who liked to sing, Mick Ronson, Mick Woodmansey, Trevor Bolder and Mark Carr-Prichard both of Arnold Corns. Obviously having a good time, they played songs from the forthcoming 'Hunky Dory' album including 'Kooks' and 'Queen Bitch'. George Underwood sang 'Song For Bob Dylan' which David had written for him and Dana Gillespie sang David's 'Andy Warhol'. The next time David surfaced was to do a late summer tour of Holland, Belgium and France in September. 'Hunky Dory' was released in December, aimed at the Christmas market.

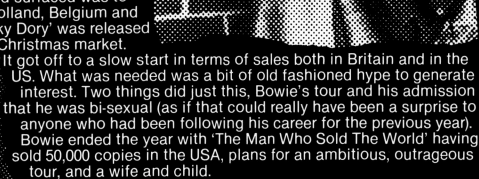

It got off to a slow start in terms of sales both in Britain and in the US. What was needed was a bit of old fashioned hype to generate interest. Two things did just this, Bowie's tour and his admission that he was bi-sexual (as if that could really have been a surprise to anyone who had been following his career for the previous year).

Bowie ended the year with 'The Man Who Sold The World' having sold 50,000 copies in the USA, plans for an ambitious, outrageous tour, and a wife and child.

David described 'Hunky Dory' as a bit 'lightweight' to one interviewer and in Disc he told Rosalind Russell 'I've got a lot out of my system, a lot of the schizophrenia. It's on a level I can't think about now. 'Hunky Dory' was a very worried album because I didn't know what I was supposed to be doing. I dared to hope too long about England, so I don't dare to hope for more. If I wasn't doing this I don't know what I'd do — I'd either be in a nuthouse or in prison.'

'Hunky Dory'
RCA SF 8244.   Released December 1971.
Producer: Ken Scott (assisted by the actor).
Arranger: Tracks 1, 4-7, Mick Ronson.
Studio: Trident, London.
1. **Changes** (Bowie)
2. **Oh! You Pretty Things** (Bowie) / **Eight Line Poem** (Bowie)
3. **Life On Mars** Bowie)
4. **Kooks** (Bowie)
5. **Quicksand** (Bowie)
6. **Fill Your Heart** (Biff Rose, Paul Williams) / **Andy Warhol** (Bowie)
7. **Song For Bob Dylan** (Bowie)
8. **Queen Bitch** (Bowie)
9. **The Bewlay Brothers** (Bowie)
David Bowie: Vocals, guitar, sexophones, piano.
Mick Ronson: Guitar
Woody Woodmansey: Drums.
Trevor Bolder: Bass, trumpets.
Richard Wakeman: Piano.

RCA   VICTOR

DAVID BOWIE
HUNKY DORY

'Our new stage act will be outrageous', David told George Tremlett, 'quite outrageous but very theatrical. It's going to be costumed and choreographed, quite different to anything anyone else has tried to do before ... No-one has ever seen anything like this before.

'It's going to be entertainment. That's what's missing in pop music now, entertainment. There's not much outrageousness left in pop music any more. There's only me and Marc Bolan. The Beatles were outrageous at one time and so was Mick Jagger — but you can't remain at the top for five years and still be outrageous ... you become accepted and the impact is gone. Me, I'm fantastically outrageous. I like being outrageous. I believe people want to see you if you're being outrageous — and I'm old enough to remember Mick Jagger!'

But even before he opened his outrageous new tour at the Lanchester Festival on January 30th, something else happened which made him the focus of attention, not just of the music press but of the news hounds of Fleet Street as well. In an interview with Michael Watts in Melody Maker of January 22nd, David admitted that he was gay.

In an interview entitled 'Oh You Pretty Thing', in Melody Maker January 22nd, Michael Watts published the fact that David was gay, or at least bi-sexual. 'David's present image is to come on like a swishy queen, a gorgeously effeminate boy. He's as camp as a row of tents with his limp hand and trolling vocabulary. 'I'm gay', he says, 'and always have been, even when I was David Jones'. But there's a sly jollity about how he says it, a secret smile at the corners of his mouth. He knows that in these times it's permissible to act like a male tart and that to shock and outrage, which pop has always striven to do throughout its history, is a ball breaking business.'

Watts asked him why he wasn't wearing his girl's dress. 'Oh dear', David replied, 'You must understand that it's not a woman's, it's a man's dress. The important fact is that I don't have to drag up. I want to go on like this for long after the fashion has finished. I'm just a cosmic yob I suppose. I've always worn my own style of clothes. I design them. I just don't like the clothes that you buy in shops. I don't wear dresses all the time either. I change every day. I'm not outrageous, I'm David Bowie.'

The admission of gayness, set in context by Michael Watts, was seized upon by Fleet Street in a paroxism of joy. If they had only opened their eyes, it must have been apparent what was happening. David had been wearing dresses for almost two years before this article. His live performances had become de rigeur for the London gay community. David had appeared in a dress on an album sleeve and made lots of swishy remarks to the press on his promo tour of the USA. It was just that no-one had dared to print it before.

Of course, whether or not all this was just part of the Tony De Fries marketing ploy is another matter. By January 1972 they already had 'Ziggy Stardust' on tape and had planned a tour that was designed to take the world by storm. A little controversy never hurt when you have an album and a tour to promote.

He described what happened when the paper hit the stands in a later interview: 'The only thing it ever did was sell albums. As soon as the article came out in Melody Maker people rang up and said, 'Don't buy the paper. You know what you've gone and done? You've just ruined yourself'. They said, 'You told him you were a bisexual', I said, 'I know. He asked me! Nobody is going to be offended by that. Everybody knows that most people are bisexual'. And I bought the paper and it looked all right. But from then on, the way the other papers picked up on it and just tore at it like dogs at meat! They made this enormous thing out of it.'

45

1972

So, in a blaze of publicity, Bowie began his first tour in two years. On the road with him were the same group that backed him on 'Hunky Dory': Mick Ronson on guitar, Woody Woodmansey on drums and Trevor Bolder on bass and trumpet. They opened at the Lanchester Festival on January 30th. He described his feelings a few days before the gig: 'I'm looking forward to going out again. I want to assert myself again as a performer and not just a writer. I'm not writing for anyone else, I never do. I think it's going to be good fun doing this. We're trying to give it the benefit of the doubt here rather than throw everything out of the window. We still don't want to do London yet. It's been a long while since I've been out and I'm taking things gradually.'

The tour continued on to the USA, then Japan, Brazil, Mexico and Europe. At least that was the plan. Angie and Zowie went along too.

The plans for a world tour were delayed. David spent time producing other artists and then went out on a British tour in June. Though many of the venues were half empty David received standing ovations wherever he went. The show was amazing. The audiences were knocked out from the moment he hit the stage in his multi-coloured jump suit with close cropped carrot coloured hair. Gone was the long haired acoustic guitarist, this was a hard rock show with The Spiders From Mars really cranking up the volume. De Fries had also very wisely spent big money to make sure the sound was perfect — something the reviewers commented favourably on. David changed his outfit three times in the show and as well as performing 'Ziggy Stardust' material he included 'Space Oddity', played as a duet by David and Mick Ronson, Cream's 'I Feel Free', and Lou Reed's 'White Light'. The audience rushed the stage at Tyneside.

The tour was a triumph. They eventually wound up in London and played Imperial College where the crowd was so ecstatic that they carried David out of the hall on their shoulders while, dressed in shiny satin trousers and white silk top, he continued to sing his encore.

'You know I never do anything by half' said David.

July 8th, 1972, can be said to be the beginning of David's superstardom. The occasion was a concert at The Royal Festival Hall at the 'Save The Whale' concert arranged by Friends of The Earth. The success can be judged from the reviews: 'Bowie Saves The Whale and Rock' headlined Disc, 'David Bowie will soon become the greatest entertainer Britain has ever known' said the normally business-like Music Week, 'Anybody still unconvinced that David Bowie will sweep all before him should have witnessed the end of his remarkable concert last Saturday' said NME, 'T.S. Eliot with a rock and roll beat' reported The Times. Melody Maker described it perfectly, under the headline 'A Star Is Born' Ray Coleman wrote, 'When a shooting star is heading for the peak, there is usually one concert at which it's possible to declare, 'That's it — he's made it'.

The show was a triumph. David varied the pace, even slowing down to do a solo version of Jacques Brel's 'Amsterdam'. At the end of the set he brought Lou Reed onstage to perform 'White Light/White Heat', 'I'm Waiting For My Man' and 'Sweet Jane'. It was Reed's first ever British appearance but even that didn't stop it being Bowie's night.

July was a busy time for David and Mick Ronson. They produced a single Mott The Hoople, a Bowie composition 'All The Young Dudes' and were making the preparations for an album. Later in the month they went into Trident Studios to begin work on 'Transformer', Lou Reed's second solo album. It was co-produced by David and Mick.

They then went on to produce an album for Mott The Hoople. David talked about it in an interview with Charles Shaar Murray:

'Everything was wrong for them, everything was terrible and because they were so down I thought I was going to have to contribute a lot of material. Now they're in a wave of optimism and they've written everything on the album bar one Lou Reed number and the 'Dudes' single I did for them.

'They were being led in so many different directions because of general apathy with their management and recording company. Everybody was very excited about them when they first came out and then because they didn't click immediately, it fell away. When I first saw them, and that wasn't very long ago, I couldn't believe that a band so full of integrity and a really very naive exuberance could command such an enormous following and not be talked about.

'The reactions at their concerts were superb and it's sad that nothing was done about them. They were breaking up. I mean, they broke up for three days and I caught them just in time and put them together again because in fact all the kids love them.'

The Lou Reed number was 'Sweet Jane', recorded with Reed actually singing the guide vocals to enable Ian Hunter to pick up the correct phrasing.

Bowie's involvement with Mott The Hoople was more extensive than just producing an album. In February 1972, after four albums for Island and with a mass of debts, they were feeling very low. Just before leaving for a tour of Switzerland they went to the studios to cut some more tracks and waiting for them was a package containing a demo tape and a note which read: 'A song for you to hear. Hope you'll ring some time and tell me what you think. David Bowie.' The number was 'Suffragette City', they played it, liked it and recorded it. They then left for Switzerland. It was in Switzerland that they became really depressed with their situation and decided to break up. On return Overend 'Pete' Watts called David to thank him for the tape and ask him if he needed a bass player. David was horrified to hear that they'd broken up and explained that he had been in the same position just before he met Tony De Fries. He would call back. Within minutes they had an appointment with De Fries and Bowie at De Fries's Mainman offices. During the meeting David sang them 'All The Young Dudes', saying 'That might do the trick.'

Tony De Fries signed them, negotiated their release from Island Records and signed them to CBS Records with CBS, a little reluctantly, paying off their past debts. David on his side agreed to produce them and together they laid down twenty tracks, all written by Ian Hunter and Mick Ralphs, with the exception of 'All The Young Dudes' by Bowie and 'Sweet Jane' by Lou Reed. Mick Ronson was to co-produce.

In an interview with George Tremlett Mick Ralphs described what it was like making the album: 'It was a revelation working with Bowie. He's a much more together bloke than most people believe he is. He has a very firm sense of direction, total control over his own career, and he knows exactly where he's going. And yet at the same time he is always looking for new ideas — not just big ideas but little improvements, little ways of doing things better.

'He works very closely with Mick Ronson and they are both very imaginative. Before recording us they both came to see us on tour and to see the way we performed on stage — because they were anxious not to project us different to the way we were.

'Then, when we were recording in the studio, David was always looking for ways of making the sound that much better, for bringing out greater clarity or using a different sound effect — some of them very strange. When we were recording the album he brought a blacksmith's anvil down to the studio one day. He had decided that he wanted the sound you get when you strike

50

(PHOTO: PICTORIAL PRESS)

an anvil with a hammer. But instead of using the studio equipment to get something close to it he got the real thing.'

July also saw David and Mick Ronson starting work on Lou Reed's album 'Transformer'. Lou had been dissatisfied with Richard Robinson's work on his first solo album and came to London to work with David and Mick. Ronson described their approach: 'We are concentrating on the feeling rather than the technical side of the music. He is an interesting person but I never know what he is thinking. However, as long as we can reach him musically it's all right.'

Bowie mania was growing but it wasn't being reflected in record sales, so, in less than five months since 'Hunky Dory' they decided to release 'The Rise And Fall Of Ziggy Stardust And The Spiders From Mars' which they had been keeping in the can for six months. It was hailed by the critics as his masterpiece. Media attention was intense but essentially limited to those critics who were part of the Bowie cult, particularly in America. De Fries put the next part of his plan for world domination into action and together with RCA Records decided to fly two dozen American media biggies to London to see David perform in concert. They would spend a weekend at the Inn On The Park and have an opportunity to meet him.

This quickly became the heaviest press trip of all time and the jostling for tickets was intense. The problem being that De Fries and RCA were aiming at the straight publications like the New York Times in order to expand Bowie's media acceptance in the States but of course the journalists who had all along supported Bowie thought that they should go as reward for their loyalty. Eventually a compromise was worked out by adding more tickets and the loyal journalists who couldn't afford to be alienated waited at JFK on a hot July Thursday, alongside critics from The New York Times, After Dark and Playboy.

Because of the time difference they arrived on the Friday which gave them a day to recover and sightsee before the Saturday night concert. The gig that had been chosen as a media presentation was at Friars Club in Aylesbury. It holds 2,000 and was packed. The alla marcia of Beethoven's Ninth Symphony came over the PA and David leapt onstage in a luminous green jumpsuit and blazing orange hair. The set had been changed and was now built entirely around the 'Ziggy' theme. David and the Spiders *were* Ziggy and the Spiders with Ronson in platinum and red sequins. It was an impressive set brought to a head, as it were, by David going down on Ronson's guitar during the final encore of 'Suffragette City'.

The stunt paid-off and the journalists were well satisfied that Bowie was indeed worth all the hoopla and hype that was going on. But more was yet to come for them. The next day David held open house at the Dorchester Hotel. Iggy Pop was there with silver hair, eye shadow and a Marc Bolan T-shirt. Lou Reed and his band were there with Lou interrupting one of David's interviews to go over and kiss him full on the mouth. Angie Bowie was there, who, after being bitten in the stomach by Reed's road manager Ernie, in turn sank her teeth into the generously proportioned left breast of Australian rock historian and columnist, the late Lillian Roxan. It was that kind of press event. David relaxed in the middle of all the madness in shades and maroon nail varnish, periodically leaving the room to change his outfit. Journalists wandered in and out talking to The Spiders, Iggy, Angie, anyone from the Ziggy circus. De Fries hovered near David, controlling the flow of visitors.

Throughout all this David gave a series of serious interviews including one to Charles Shaar Murrey where they began talking about the use of theatre in rock. David talked about it at length: 'If we have a theatricality it comes through from us as people not as a set environment or

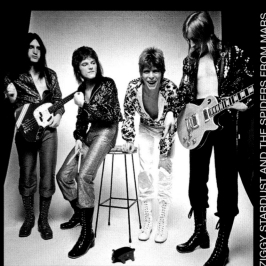

stage. Like playing an instrument theatre craftsmanship is something that one learns. There are going to be a lot of tragedies and a lot of clangers dropped over the next few years when a lot of bands try to become theatrical without knowing their craft. I'm a very professional person and I feel that I contribute all my energy into my stage performance, that when I'm on stage I give more to an audience than to anybody else when I'm off stage. I've worked hard at it. I was with a mime company and I've had other theatre experience.

'What I'm trying to say is that it's as important to know about the things you do and to have learnt it as it is to learn your instrument. As the theatrical expression evolves a lot of it is going to be on a secondary modern school amateur dramatics level. There will only be the odd few bands who have the knowledge to master their theatre.

'Iggy has natural theatre. It's very interesting because it doesn't conform to any standards or rules or structures of theatre. It's his own and it's just a Detroit Theatre that he's brought with him. It's straight from the street.

'Remember we have only been on the road for three months, so it's still coming together. But I wish myself to be a prop, if anything, for my own songs. I want to be the vehicle for my songs. I would like to colour the material with as much visual expression as is necessary for that song.'

'Ziggy Stardust' had advance sales of 150,000 in the UK alone. Things were going just as De Fries planned them. He put into operation the next stage of the plan. No more interviews. It is the oldest trick in the world but it worked. The music press squealed with rage at having their Ziggy taken away from them. Interest in David soared, every tiny detail that leaked out, whether it was about his private hairdresser or the name of the man who made his boots was lovingly reported. And all this time David, Angie and their son Zowie were living in their £7 a week flat in Beckenham. The ultimate show was being planned. One in which David actually became Ziggy.

David brought in Lindsay Kemp to help organise the stage presentation, and planned a spectacular in the Busby Berkeley tradition. The set was constructed of different levels of scaffolding so that David could appear on different levels in different outfits. He was aided onstage by not only The Spiders From Mars but by Mathew Fisher on keyboards and Lindsay Kemp and a dance troup called The Astronettes. There was a light show and dry ice and costumes ... It was the most extravagant rock show ever performed in Britain. They rehearsed for two weeks at the Theatre Royale in Stratford East before the concert which was held at The Rainbow Theatre on August 19th, simply billed as 'Ziggy Stardust'.

It was his most theatrical venture so far. From the opening moments when he appeared out of the darkness, striding through dry ice to sing 'Lady Stardust' while the face of Marc Bolan was projected by his side to the grand finale with David joining The Astronettes in a frenzied dance. The show was described by Lou Reed as 'amazing, stupendous, incredible — the greatest thing I've ever seen.' But this view was not universal. Many of the audience suffered from overkill and could still not accept the total theatre side of their hero: things like the slightly overweight Lindsay Kemp wearing a pair of wings and smoking a joint while David sings 'Starman', ending it with a half sobbing rendition of 'Over The Rainbow' made them distinctly nervous.

In a breakfast interview the day before The Rainbow show, David talked to Andrew Tyler about his Ziggy Stardust persona: 'I think what I do and the way I dress is me pandering to my own eccentricities and imagination. It's a continual fantasy. Nowadays there is really no

Changes (Bowie) / **Andy Warhol** (Bowie)
RCA 2160.   Released January 7, 1972.
Producer: Ken Scott (assisted by the actor.)
Starman (Bowie) / **Suffragette City** (Bowie)
RCA 2199.   Released April 14, 1972.
Producers: David Bowie, Ken Scott.

'Revelations: A Musical Anthology for Glastonbury Fayre'
Revelation Records REV 1/2/3 (triple album with several booklets and posters)
Released April 1972 in an edition of 5,000 copies.
Record 2, Side 1, Band 3:
Supermen
Produced by Tony Visconti
Recorded live at Trident Studios, London.
David Bowie: Acoustic guitar and vocals.
Mick Ronson: Lead guitar.
Mick Woodmansey: Drums.
Trevor Bolder: Bass.

(PHOTO: MICK ROCK, PICTORIAL PRESS)

'The Rise and Fall of Ziggy Stardust and the Spiders from Mars'
RCA SF 8287.   Released June 1972.
Producers: David Bowie, Ken Scott.
Arrangers: David Bowie, Mick Ronson.
Studio: Trident, London.
1. **Five Years** (Bowie)
2. **Soul Love** (Bowie)
3. **Moonage Daydream** (Bowie)
4. **Starman** (Bowie)
5. **It Ain't Easy** (Bowie)
6. **Lady Stardust** (Bowie)
7. **Star** (Bowie)
8. **Hang On To Yourself** (Bowie)
9. **Ziggy Stardust** (Bowie)
10. **Suffragette City** (Bowie)
11. **Rock 'n' Roll Suicide** (Bowie)
David Bowie: Guitar, saxophone, vocals.
Mick Ronson: Guitar, piano, vocals.
Trevor Bolder: Bass.
Mick Woodmansey: Drums.

difference between my personal life and anything I do onstage. I'm very rarely David Jones anymore. I think I've forgotten who David Jones is.

'I really don't know what we're doing. If we're the spearhead of anything, we're not necessarily the spearhead of anything good. But people like Lou and I are probably predicting the end of an era and I mean that catastrophically. Any society that allows people like Lou and I to become rampant is pretty well lost.

'I've always been very scared about what I represent and very wary of being categorised because I'm not altogether very sure of what I represent. I'm a ball of confusion, mentally, physically ... everything about me is confused and Lou is very much the same way. We're both very mixed up, paranoid people — absolute walking messes — and Iggy's as bad.'

In the same interview he spelled out where the name of Ziggy Stardust had come from. 'It's wholly derivative, an archetype, a cliché.' The Ziggy comes from Iggy Pop and/or Twiggy and the Stardust from The Legendary Stardust Cowboy, a C&W singer on the US Mercury label who once appeared on Laugh-In who walked off and cried because the audience laughed at him, not realising that he meant what he was doing.

In August David produced Lou Reed's 'Transformer' at Trident Studios in Soho.

'Do you know how I met Iggy — and Lou Reed? I was at an RCA party at Max's Kansas City in New York and was introduced to Lou. He immediately started telling me some story about a guy who injected smack through his forehead — that's typical Lou.

'Anyway, up comes this funny ragged, ragged little guy with broken teeth and Lou says 'Don't talk to him, he's a junkie' — that was Iggy. You can't help loving him, he's so vulnerable.'

On September 1st RCA released David's new single, 'John I'm Only Dancing' and he did a small tour of Britain prior to leaving for a massive US tour. His was the first concert to be held at Manchester's new purpose-built Hardrock Concert Theatre, a 3,500 seater hall that was one of the first in the UK designed for rock music. He surprised the audience by doing a restrained set with none of the really grand excesses. He still got the audience on its feet, particularly for the new single.

When he appeared at the Top Rank Suite in Hanley the management were inspired to invent a lurid green Ziggy cocktail for the occasion.

David slid into the States on the QE2 in mid-September and did warm-up concerts in Cleveland, Ohio and Memphis, Tennessee before returning to New York City for his crucial Carnegie Hall concert.

It was to be the tour of tours, financed by RCA Records, a glittering retinue of roadies, publicists Cherry Vanilla and Tony Zanetta, chauffeurs, David's personal hairdresser Sue Fussey, The Spiders From Mars, Angie, and assorted retainers, all protected by the tightest security system that the industry had ever seen. The press couldn't get into press conferences. Bouncers at back-stage parties had instructions to let no-one through at all, on one occasion the support band were thrown out of back stage two minutes before they were due to go on and had to telephone the promoter before they could do their act.

September 28th, a Thursday night, was the date of David's New York City debut. The concert was at the prestigious old Carnegie Hall. This was the occasion where David was going to have to prove himself worth all the hype and publicity. A single Klieg light stood outside the hall, lighting the sky as if for a Hollywood premier. The audience arrived dressed in velvet and lace, sequins and glitter, men in dresses, dangerously high heels, sprayed-on face masks, it

John I'm Only Dancing (Bowie) / **Hang On To Yourself** (Bowie)
RCA 2263.   Released September 1, 1972.
Producers: Side A, David Bowie for Mainman.
Side B, David Bowie, Ken Scott for Gem.
This version of 'John I'm Only Dancing' was re-made during the 'Aladdin Sane' sessions. This re-make was used on the 'Changesone-bowie' compilation album and when the single was re-issued it was the new version that was used. Therefore only early pressings of RCA 2263 have the original version.
'Changesonebowie' was then changed to include the first version instead of the re-make so effectively the album now contains the single and the single contains the album track. In 1979 RCA confused the issue even more by issuing a 12" single with a third version of 'John I'm Only Dancing' cut at the 'Young Americans' session and being a six-minute disco version. The B side of the 1979 release is the original 1972 single release.

DAVID WITH MICK RONSON (PHOTO: ROGER PERRY)

DAVID WITH IGGY POP AND LOU REED

was trash and chic night. The Warhol contingent were there. The New York Dolls and their weird followers, and the World press. Every one of the British music papers had a correspondent there and then there was the New York press, getting ready for the show in the bar of the Cafe Carnegie. Ticket touts were selling $6 tickets for $30.

David, just to make it even more like a movie, had contracted a 48 hour flu virus and should really have been in bed. Singer Ruth Copeland opened the show but though she was loud, not too many people were in their seats to see her, they were too busy looking at each other in the lobby. Then, after the intermission came the familiar Clockwork Orange/Beethoven introduction and in a burst of light from three strobe lights, The Spiders From Mars were on stage, assisted by pianist Mike Garrison from NY. Then there was Bowie, plugging in a jumbo 12 string.

His set was similar to the one which had wowed the American journalists in Aylesbury. From 'Ziggy Stardust' came 'Hang On', 'Lady Stardust', 'Moonage Daydream', 'Five Years', 'Starman', and 'Suffragette City'. From 'Hunky Dory' came 'Changes', 'Life On Mars', 'Queen Bitch' and, with his subject in the audience, 'Andy Warhol'. The security was so tight that Andy couldn't even get a backstage pass. His acoustic interlude included the Jacques Brel 'Port of Amsterdam' and 'Space Oddity'. 'This is like bringing coals to Newcastle' he announced as he went into the two Lou Reed numbers, 'I'm Waiting For My Man' and 'White Light/White Heat'. The bass amp blew out during the latter but the group kept on rocking. He chose Chuck Berry's 'Round and Round' as his encore.

The tour was so successful that RCA and De Fries decided to extend it by another eight weeks. He had arrived with eight concerts booked, now they added another seventeen including Houston, New Orleans, Kansas City, Phoenix, Miami, Atlanta, Salt Lake City, Denver, Saint Louis, Oklahoma City, Nashville, San Francisco, Cincinnati, Seattle, Louisville, Indianapolis and Dallas. And so the crazy travelling circus meandered across the States with David adding new songs to the set as he wrote them from the back of his bus. Later the bus was replaced by trains as the distances became too great but he was still enclosed in the cocoon of tight security created by De Fries. No-one could get in.

One of the songs written on the Greyhound was 'The Jean Genie'. As the tour snaked across the country he recorded it at the RCA studios in New York City, Nashville and Los Angeles. The masters were then flown to London for November 24th release. The press were excluded completely from the tour bus and had to go on ahead under their own steam. Tony De Fries explained his attitude to security to Timothy Ferris of Rolling Stone who, having finally met Bowie, devoted a four page spread to the meeting.

De Fries: 'If you're taking a performer who's going to be the most important artist in his area within a very short space of time — which has already happened to Bowie in England — then you find yourself dealing with an audience who want to get *to* your artist by *whatever means possible*. If you don't have security the artist suffers because you get break-ins, riots, people hurt and all that sort of thing. This is not going to happen to Bowie if I can help it.'

De Fries went on to very accurately predict Bowie's future career. 'Bowie is setting a standard in rock 'n' roll which other people are going to have to get to if they want to stay around in the seventies. I think he's very much a seventies artist. I think most of the artists who are with us at the moment are sixties artists and Bowie, certainly to me, is going to be a major artist of the seventies. In 1975 he will be at his peak in music. What he does after that is going to depend on his talents in other fields. I want to see him on film. I want to see him in feature films ...'

Do Anything You Say (Bowie) / **I Dig
Everything** (Bowie) // Can't Help Thinking
About Me / I'm Not Losing Sleep (Bowie)
Pye 7NX 8002.   Released October 6, 1972.
An Extended Play, 33⅓, compilation of 1966
Pye singles tracks.

The Jean Genie (Bowie) / **Ziggy Stardust**
(Bowie)
RCA 2302.   Released November 24, 1972.
Producers: Side A, David Bowie for Mainman.
Side B, David Bowie, Kenn Scott for Gem.

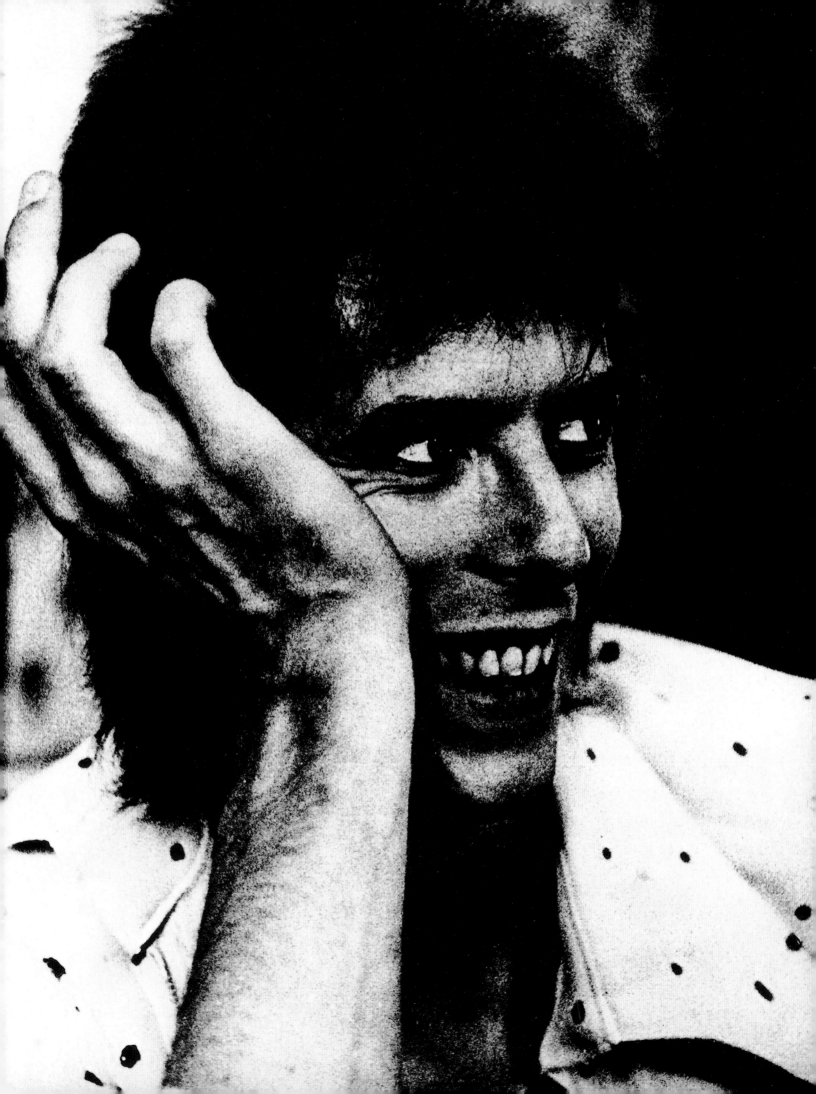

David returned to Britain for Christmas and on January 17th recorded a show for London Weekend TV's 'Russell Harty Plus'. His eyebrows have been replaced by finely sketched red lines and he was wearing red eyeshadow. He sang 'Drive-In Saturday', a number premiered on the US tour at Fort Lauderdale, Florida, and a selection of other numbers from his show including Jacques Brel's 'My Death'.

David had added new musicians to the lineup but explained that they were not new Spiders, 'The Spiders are still Trevor, Woody and Mick; we've just got in some backup men on tenor saxes and piano and voices. I'm concentrating mainly on the music and I shall work on the theatrics of the thing if I have enough time, because I never believe that time can be eaten away as quickly as it is when we're working as we are at the moment.'

The schedule was tight. David had to finish his new album, 'Aladdin Sane' by January 24th and then sail to New York City, get in two weeks of rehearsals and open the second American tour at New York's Radio City on February 14th — a Valentine's Day concert. He talked about America.

'We were kept very much to ourselves in America and we were very wary of America the first time. Next time we may be able to get out and about a bit more. We were very paranoid about it.'

In the same interview he also talked about his new character, 'Aladdin Sane'; 'I don't think Aladdin is as clearly cut and well-defined a character as Ziggy was. Ziggy was meant to be clearly cut and well-defined with areas for interplay, whereas Aladdin is pretty ephemeral. He's also a situation as opposed to just being an individual. I think he encompasses situations as well as just being a personality.'

As well as recording 'Aladdin Sane' he put the finishing touches to Lou Reed's 'Transformer' album which was to re-establish Reed's career and even give him his first hit single, the unlikely 'Walk On The Wild Side' albeit in a highly edited form.

The album completed, David left Southampton on January 25th on board the QE2 to start a 100 day world tour.

The Radio City concert was a cause of much speculation in New York with many people expecting him to simply restage the spectacular Rainbow show for an American audience. David outdid himself. Before a crowd of 6,200 people, a single spotlight picked out a figure imprisoned in a silver cage some fifty feet above the stage. As David stared out into the audience the cage began its perilous descent and the band crashed into 'Hang On To Yourself' — a very appropriate number considering David's great fear of heights. It was a very fast paced show, not allowing the audience one minute to catch their breath before a new number began with a whole plethora of new effects. Silver spheres span either side of the stage and to open the second half of the show David and the Spiders rose up out of the stage trapdoor as if they had been beamed down from Starship Enterprise. The numbers included a lot of new material from the as yet unreleased 'Aladdin Sane' album and some familiar numbers had been totally changed. 'Space Oddity' was no longer the acoustic duet between David and Mick — now it was a full production number and even included a Mellotron.

They did the Stones' 'Let's Spend The Night Together', 'The Jean Genie', closed with 'Suffragette City' and did 'Rock 'n' Roll Suicide' as an encore. David managed to make five costume changes during the show.

At the end of the show David fainted. A nurse took his blood pressure and diagnosed

overwork. He slept a solid twelve hours.

This tour was even more extravagant than the last. Sue Fussey was still with him to dress his hair but now he also had a personal dresser named Freddie, a black bodyguard, and Pierre LaRoche from The House of Arden travelling with him to do his makeup. It was a far cry from travelling round in a beat up old ambulance. This time when they arrived in Hollywood David stayed at The Beverley Hills Hotel while the Spiders had to make do with The Continental Hyatt House.

While David was away touring in The States, his past came back to haunt him in the form of 'The Image', the movie he made way back in 1967. It was shown at The Jacey, Trafalgar Square, sandwiched between 'I Am Sexy' and 'Erotic Blue'.

On April 6th 'Drive In Saturday' was released as a single. It went into the top five on the British charts. It was written during a night train journey while crossing the great desert region between Seattle and Phoenix, Arizona. David caught sight of some strange silver domes on the horizon and, as no-one on the train knew what they were, David's imagination set to work. The song is set somewhere in the future.

The album 'Aladdin Sane' was released by RCA with advance sales of 100,000 copies — the first time anyone had achieved that since The Beatles. The songs were all written during his first tour of America the previous autumn. As the train zigzagged across the continent Bowie scribbled down his impressions. It has been commented that this was his 'On The Road' since he was so influenced by Kerouac's book when he was a teenager. David spoke of it, 'I think the biggest thing that hit me about America is that I feel the American is the loneliest person in the world. I get an awful feeling of general insecurity and a need for warmth in people. It's sad, very sad. I think so many people are unaware that they are living in America. I think they hear about America. There are *very* few Americans who are aware they are *in* America. It's a bit serious isn't it?'

So the songs on the album were written all over The States: 'Watch That Man' was from New York, the title track 'Aladdin Sane 1913-1938-197?' was written on the liner Ellinis on the way back to Britain for Christmas. 'Drive In Saturday' in the desert between Seattle and Phoenix, 'Panic In Detroit' was from Detroit and 'The Cracked Actor' was written in Los Angeles. 'Time' comes from New Orleans and 'The Jean Genie' was written in New York and Detroit. Two others come from London: 'The Prettiest Star' was written in Gloucester Road while 'Lady Grinning Soul' was written about American soul singer Claudia Lennear. Not only did she inspire David to write about her charms but Mick Jagger wrote 'Brown Sugar' about her, a modern day Misha.

The new version of 'John I'm Only Dancing' was originally scheduled for the album but was left off at the last minute. The original sound track list also contained a song called 'Zion' which 'Lady Grinning Soul' replaced.

After an extended US tour, the Bowie caravan next appeared in Japan where he did ten concerts in April. He toured the country as a tourist while he was there in order to see ritual dance performances. 'There was an awful lot, particularly in the outlying villages and provinces, of very strange ritual dance performances that I hadn't seen before. I never really found out from what school it came or what its origins were. A lot of them were from Shintoism ...' The Japanese trip had a considerable impact on David. Years later he was to play koto on 'Moss Garden' ('Heroes') and there are lyrics about Japan on 'Blackout' on the same

DAVID WITH ANGIE (PHOTO: PICTORIAL PRESS)

album. While he was there he had Kansai, the famous Japanese fashion designer design an entire wardrobe of extravagant stage clothes for him. David's own impact on Japan is harder to see. David admitted later that the Japanese seemed to find his show barely comprehensible.

'In Japan when we were faced with an audience that we presumed didn't understand a word of what I was saying — there I was more physical than on any other tour I've ever done and I carried it over back here again. Literally I activated the whole thing with my hands and my body. I needn't have sung half the time.

'In America we'll just keep it down to simplicities. But Americans are very academic towards their rock and need it to have a cultural stability. The Japanese are theatrical and far more aware than either England or America, and England is at still another end of the spectrum.

'It's not the theatre they want, it's not the academics they want, it's just the rock concert. Because we do each of them so fast, it's nice to move from one country to another.

'The biggest difference is Japan. In England and America I play more or less the same way. Possibly in America we play a much harder set. Even though the Americans are more inclined towards this cultural thing, they need it to be more primitive.'

The trip continued. On April 21st he left Japan for Moscow on the Trans-Siberian Express. After two days in Moscow he took the express to Paris. 'Russia is an impossible country to talk about. It's so vast. The people we found to be warm, generally. When we got to Moscow they were colder.'

David and Angie spent the night at the Georges Cinq in Paris and then missed the morning train after travelling 7,900 miles to catch it. However there was another to Boulogne where they took the hovercraft to Dover. There were over three hundred girls waiting for him at Victoria Station. Police bustled him into the waiting limousine and he was soon back in his £7 a week flat in Beckenham.

David had been Ziggy full time for nine months and the strain was telling. He spoke to Melody Maker on arrival in Britain. 'I'm sick of being Gulliver. You know, after America, Moscow, Siberia, Japan ... I just want to bloody well go home to Beckenham and watch the telly. This decadence thing is just a bloody joke. I'm very normal. I am me and I have to carry on with what I've started. There is nothing else for me to do. I have been under a great strain though. For me, performing is indeed a great strain. I've also become disillusioned with certain things. I never believed a hype could be made of an artist before that artist had got anywhere. That's what happened you see. But when I saw that our albums were really selling I knew that one period was over. The hype was over. Well, it wasn't but at least we'd done something to be hyped about.

'But that whole hype thing at the start was a monster to endure. It hurt me quite a lot. I had to go through a lot of crap. I mean, I never thought Ziggy would become the most talked about man in the world. I never thought it would become that unreal.

'The characters I have written about have indeed been the roles I have wished to portray. Ziggy — that dead creature. I loved him. I feel somewhat like a Doctor Frankenstein. Although Ziggy follows David Bowie very closely, they are indeed two people. What have I created?

'Ziggy hit the nail on the head. He just came at the rightest, ripest time ... I know I have created a somewhat strange audience — but that audience is also full of little Noddy Holders and little Iggy Pops. I know we used to attract a load of queens at one stage but then other factions of people crept in. Now you can't tell anymore. They're all there for some reason. And

we get young people. Those lovely young people. And they have to be considered very seriously. They cannot be forgotten — as they might be. We cannot afford to lose them by continuing to make rock a cultural force. We must not leave the young behind. I repeat that. You see I don't want to aim statements at them. Again, the whole idea of being a statesman is abhorrent to me.'

David's first show back in Britain was ill-advisedly held at Earls Court Stadium. The barest minimum had been spent on the show by the promoters: the stage was low so that most of the audience couldn't see a thing and the sound system was terrible with most of the hall being full of quadrophonic echo. The audience, some of whom had paid up to £25 to scalpers for a ticket, naturally pushed their way down to the front to try and see their hero. A group of four Australians, having consumed a formidable amount of Southern Comfort, ripped off their clothes and began dancing naked in the aisle. A young woman objected and slapped one of them across the face. Things turned ugly when he retaliated by ripping her blouse off. Another young man began urinating in the aisle and eventually several hundred people were scuffling and shouting. The concert was stopped and David appealed to the audience to 'stop being silly.' After ten minutes the show restarted but the kids again left their seats and crowded to the front because they couldn't hear or see. The promoters had sold 18,000 seats at £2 a ticket and later admitted that all the complaints were justified. The concert however was a flop with many people leaving before the end. David was so upset that he cancelled the show he was due to perform at Earls Court on June 30th.

After Earls Court David began the biggest tour that Britain had ever seen. It opened on May 16th at The Music Hall in Aberdeen. He arrived by train, ten hours from London. The show had sold out and another was quickly organised. Sound check at 5 pm, first show at 7 pm, the second at 9 pm. The beginning of what was to become routine for the next two months. The next day he played Caird Hall in Dundee, then still staying in Scotland played Green's Playhouse in Glasgow on May 18th and The Empire Theatre, Edinburgh on the 19th.

After the tour he recalled the Glasgow gig: 'We had I think, four couples making it in the back row which was fabulous. It's the first time I've heard of that happening. There was also a whole row of seats physically torn out of the floor, which sounds like the fifties to me. Can you imagine how much energy has to be used to tear out a theatre seat?'

After a day off, the show entered England. The circus travelled by coach and train with David protected by bodyguards and dressed and made-up by professionals. Sue Fussey still did his hair. They did Norwich Theatre Royal on May 21, Romford Odeon on May 22, Brighton Dome on May 23, Lewisham Odeon on May 24 and Bournemouth Winter Gardens on May 25, most of which were fairly easy because the tour could return to London each night. Then came Guildford Civic Hall on May 27, Wolverhampton Civic Hall on May 28 and Hanley Victoria Hall on May 29.

The six week tour was well under way by now. They played Blackburn King George's Hall on May 31, Bradford St. George's Hall on June 1st, Coventry New Theatre on June 3, Worcester Gaumont on June 4, a day off and then up north again to Sheffield City Hall on June 6, Manchester Free Trade Hall on June 7, Newcastle City Hall on June 8, Preston Guildhall on June 9, Liverpool Empire Theatre on June 10, Leicester DeMontfort Hall on June 11, Chatham Central Hall on June 12, Kilburn Gaumont on June 13, Salisbury City Hall on June 14, Taunton Odeon on June 15 and Torquay Town Hall on June 16.

he press reacted with horror at David's announcement that he was quitting but the best nalysis of what was happening came in an interview with Mick Ronson when he explained, Bowie can't be the same all the time. He has changed and things naturally become faster. Now he has to think about films. We're all going to miss the adoring crowds and the glamour hat goes with it but to continue wouldn't be right. Bowie has to become a legend — that's the only way he can last.'

David meanwhile had gone to the Chateau d'Herouville, Chopin's old place just outside Paris. This was Elton John's 'Honky Chateau' but it was Marc Bolan who recommended it to David after he recorded 'The Slider' there. The Chateau is a residential studio where artists can work any time of day or night in full comfort and with no outside distractions. David had three projects to work on: an album of sixties oldies which was released as 'Pin Ups', mixing a live album from the tapes of the last Hammersmith concert and a solo album which had a provisional title of 'Bowie-ing Out' but which, though a number of backing tracks were laid down, didn't come to anything. There were also plans for a Mick Ronson solo album which David was going to produce.

Originally David had not invited The Spiders From Mars rhythm section to come along and had asked Jack Bruce and Aynsley Dunbar to come along instead. Aynsley, fresh from playing with Frank Zappa, obliged but Bruce had other plans. Trevor Bolder was somewhat embarrassedly asked if he could come along as well. Mike Garson, the American pianist who had been with David ever since the first US tour came along as well. Garson, a Scientologist, had managed to convert Woody Woodmansey and so, while David and the ex-Spiders blasted their way through the golden oldies of the psychedelic age, Woody fiddled with the e-meters and security checks at Scientology HQ in East Grinstead.

Having retired from the road, David was now virtually inaccessible but a number of pressmen managed to see him. Only one of them got a decent interview and that, oddly, was the man from the Daily Mail, Roderick Gilchrist. David spoke at length to him about a variety of subjects, starting naturally enough with his retirement from the stage:
Believe it or not, I didn't actually want to be a rock 'n' roll star. I had an awful lot of fun doing that but the reason I went on the road was to interpret the songs I was writing in an atmosphere I felt was realistic for those songs. That was okay but my performance on stage reached a peak. I felt I couldn't go on stage in the same context again because I don't like the feeling that I am repeating myself.

'I've done America twice and I've toured all of England and Japan and I got to the point where I asked myself, 'What's the point in doing it all again?' Money? I don't have financial worries and if I'm tired with what I'm doing it wouldn't be long before the audience realised.'

'Pin Ups' was an album of British hits. The songs that had shaped David's generation of musicians. 'These are all songs that really meant a lot to me then. They're all very dear to me. These are all bands that I used to go and hear play down the Marquee between 1964 and 1967. Each one meant something to me at the time. It's my London of the time. I used to go up to town on Friday night, see what was going on, stay over for the night ...'

It was interesting that although David had all the records at home, when it came to re-recording them he purposely left them all back in England, using just the basic arrangements that they had copied out on score paper.

Also while recording at Chateau d'Herouville The Daily Mirror planned a photo feature of

had guest spots on the US TV series 'Hawaii Five-O' and 'FB.I.' and was even offered the le
in 'Wonder Woman' which Lynda Carter later took. The Daily Mirror made her 'The Woman
1974'.

With Angie so much in the limelight David was questioned about her in interviews. He to
the Daily Express, 'I think we're both fairly volatile. When we go away and experience diffe
things and come back together again it makes our lives more interesting. It's a more natur
way of living as well ... we are both very sexual. We were never faithful to each other before
got married. There's no reason to be particularly faithful to each other after we got married
would be a front. The only reason we got married was because we loved each other, not fo
sexual possession.'

Angie also spoke about their relationship in interviews. She told The Chicago Sun Times
'What we need in our marriage is space. Space when we are apart and space when we are
together. Otherwise I'd get claustrophobic. What we don't want is possessiveness.
Togetherness is a killer.

'If I am sleeping with someone and David phones me from America because he needs n
go right away. And the boy will drive me to the airport. When David and I married we were
insecure and didn't know who we were. I still don't. David had to take this leap in the dark
his career and I held his hand. Now it's my turn to take the leap.'

While David was recording 'Pin Ups', Decca rummaged around in their vaults and came
with a single from 1967, 'The Laughing Gnome', which they released to David's acute
embarrassment. With interest in David running so high it sold over 250,000 and became on
his biggest selling singles. The critics were amazed, many of them not having been around
long and not realising the many faces David Bowie took before he became Ziggy and Alad

On October 12, RCA released 'Sorrow' together with 'Amsterdam'. To the relief of many,
David hadn't entirely given up live performances. He spent three days, October 18, 19 and
on stage at The Marquee filming a concert for NBC TV's 'Midnight Special' show in the St
NBC specifically wanted to shoot it at The Marquee because of the atmosphere there. Ow
Jack Barrie was quite surprised then when the American technicians insisted on repainting
and doing a certain amount of remodelling because it wasn't photogenic enough!

With David on the show were Marianne Faithfull, who sang 'As Tears Go By' and The Tr
looking wildly out of place in a sea of transvestites, gays, glamourboys and media heavies
audience had been selected by democratic ballot from the members of the Marquee Club
of the David Bowie Fanclub. There were 200 for each of the three shows. Also allowed in w
select members of the press and of course David's friends. Tony Visconti and his wife, Ma
Hopkin were there, Lionel Bart, Dana Gillespie and Wayne County were there. Wayne wore
New York street drag of a red negligee bought in Piccadilly, a snowball wig and carrying a
metal handbag engraved with the words 'Campus Queen'. Long John Baldry, who used to
virtually live in The Marquee, mingled with Bowie fans, some of whom had been loyal since

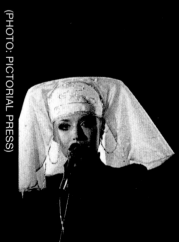

days of The King Bees. The show lasted for ninety minutes and David had originally intended to call it 'The 1980 Floor Show', as a pun on George Orwell's grim predictions. David was rumoured to be working on a musical adaptation of '1984' for the West End Stage. It never saw the light of day but much of the music saw its final form on the 'Diamond Dogs' album, particularly the song '1984' itself, which can easily be imagined as a stage mumber. Since he knew the show would be repeated in years to come David wisely presented a variety of different characters and songs. There were bits of Ziggy, some numbers from the forthcoming 'Pin Up' album and a preview of '1984'. He wore everything from a fishnet skin-tight jump suit embellished with a huge pair of jewel encrusted hands which grabbed his chest from behind, to a sci-fi corset trimmed with feathers. He did all the old favourites: 'Space Oddity', 'Time', 'Everything's All Right', 'I Can't Explain', 'The Jean Genie', and, the climax of the show, David and Marianne Faithfull singing 'I Got You, Babe' with Marianne dressed as a nun.

The filming was constantly interrupted. Most numbers had to be repeated over and over. On one the camera caught a glimpse of David's jockstrap — forbidden on US TV. On another Mick Ronson broke a string. The lineup wasn't exactly The Spiders though David introduced them as such. Ronson was there, so was Trevor Bolder on bass but Aynsley Dunbar was on drums as he was on 'Pin Ups' and David's neighbour, Mark Pritchard, was on second guitar. It was a very clever show, one which was repeated frequently on US television.

October 19th, 'Pin Ups' was finally released to advance orders of 150,000 copies. On the sleeve was a photo of David with Twiggy taken by Justin de Villeneuve. Twiggy seems to be remembering the sixties but David looks like he's just seen the future.

In December David was producing an album by his friends The Astronettes: Eve, Jason Guess and Warren Peace (Geoffrey McCormack), at Olympic Studios in Barnes. The numbers laid down were quite varied — four Bowie numbers, one of Zappa's, one of Springsteen's, The Beach Boys' 'God Only Knows' and a couple of jazz numbers. The tracks also had to have brass and string arrangements added and so Puerto Rican arranger Luis Ramirez was being specially flown in to work on it. At the same sessions David was working on new material of his own. He recorded '1984' and other tracks for the two shows he was still working on at this point: 'The Ziggy Show which comprised the music from the Ziggy Stardust album plus five new songs written for it and the '1984' show, which had 20 songs waiting for it of which he expected to use only 14. "1984' is almost a kitchen sink kind of thing and I shall look very different in it.'

The pressure of fans finally forced David and Angie, and baby Zowie, to move out of Haddon Hall. They moved into actress Diana Rigg's central London home while she was working abroad and began negotiations to buy Richard Harris's house in Kensington. They also managed to have a quick holiday in Cyprus where Angie's parents were living. At the end of 1973, RCA records revealed that in Britain alone, David sold over 1,056,400 albums and 1,024,068 singles in less than two years.

Sorrow (Feldman, Goldstein, Gottehrer) /
Amsterdam (Brel, Shuman)
RCA 2424.   Released September 28, 1973.
Producers: David Bowie, Ken Scott.
The A side is a preview from the forthcoming
'Pin Ups' album. The B side is the Jacques
Brel number.

The Laughing Gnome (Bowie) / **The Gospel
According To Tony Day** (Bowie)
Deram DM 123.   Released September 8, 1973.
Producer: Mike Vernon.
Notes: A re-issue from 1967.

DVID WITH LOU REED. (PHOTO: MICK ROCK. PICTORIAL PRESS)

'Pin Ups'
RCA RS 1003.   Released October 1973.
Producers: David Bowie, Ken Scott.
Engineer: Denis Blackeye.
1. **Rosalyn** (Duncan, Farley)
2. **Here Comes The Night** (Berns)
3. **I Wish You Would** (Billy Boy Arnold)
4. **See Emily Play** (Barrett)
5. **Everything's Alright** (Crouch, Konrad,
   Stavely, James, Karlson)
6. **I Can't Explain** (Townshend)
7. **Friday On My Mind** (Young, Vanda)
8. **Sorrow** (Feldman, Goldstein, Gottehrer)
9. **Don't Bring Me Down** (Johnnie Dee)
10. **Shapes Of Things** (Samwell-Smith,
    McCarthy)
11. **Anyway, Anyhow, Anywhere** (Townshend,
    Daltrey)
12. **Where Have All The Good Times Gone?**
David Bowie: Vocals, backing vocals, Moog
synthesizer, harmonica, tenor and alto
saxophones.
Mick Ronson: Guitar, piano, back-up vocals.
T.J. Bolder: Bass guitar.

Aynsley Dunbar: Drums.
Mike Garson: Piano, organ, harpsichord,
electric piano.
Ken Fordham: Baritone saxophone.
Mac Cormack: Back-up vocals.

January opened with Polydor releasing Lulu's version of 'The Man Who Sold The World', written by David and co-arranged and co-produced by David and Mick Ronson. David sings back-up vocals and also blows saxophone.

January also saw Mick Ronson's first solo single, 'Love Me Tender', released by RCA on January 25. The Spiders from Mars were no more and Mainman was now pushing Ronson into a solo career.

February came and David was still in Olympic Studios. He had been there almost every day and most nights since October working on various projects. It was all planned, as usual, and he had booked the time a year before. The priorities of some of his projects had changed by now as he explained to Disc journalist Fox Cumming. 'I haven't walked in the light of day for ages except from my front door to the car and again from the car into the studios.' He explained that the projected live album of the Hammersmith concert, which was to be called 'The Last Concert', had been held up because it was keyed to the film of the concert made by D.A. Pennebaker. The movie had been scheduled to premier at Leicester Square in February but 'when it appears depends on Pennebaker who is still working on the last half hour of it. His deadline was December 24, 1973 but the man's an artist, you can't tie him down to things like that. Since the film has been held up it follows that the soundtrack album will be delayed as well.' This was to be the last anyone heard of the film or album despite the fact that all the studio work on the album had been done.

Another project he had been working on had also been shelved, 'The 1980 Floorshow' which, together with 'The Ziggy Stardust Show' had occupied much of David's time since he retired from touring. 'I don't know if I shall have anything to do with either of the two musicals. I'm certainly too busy with other things at the present to be able to appear in either of them. I would like to get into a theatre run at some time but it would have to be a short one.'

He had also been toying with the idea of a 'Pin Ups 2'. 'I never intended to do a 'Pin Ups 2' but since the first one I've already found about five songs of other people's that I want to do.'

All these things had taken second place to a new studio album, based on his experiences touring the United States and the Soviet Union which had profoundly shocked and changed him. 'This one again has a theme. It's a backward look at the sixties and seventies and a very political album. My protest. These days you have to be more subtle about protesting than before. You can't preach at people any more. You have to adopt a position of almost indifference. You have to be supercool nowadays. This album is more me than anything I've done previously.' The album was to be 'Diamond Dogs'.

'Rebel, Rebel' was released on February 15, though not in the States. It was an obvious choice for England. By the end of the month David was once more crossing the Atlantic by liner ready for the launch of 'Diamond Dogs' in the States and for tough business meetings with Tony De Fries in New York.

'Diamond Dogs', with its grim prediction of urban decay and waste, despair and hopelessness, was received with mixed feelings. On the one hand all the numbers were fast and raunchy rockers but on the other hand, David's message of a Big Brother fascist future was regarded by some as the height of pretension. Tony De Fries on the other hand didn't really care which it was, he just wanted to sell it.

It had been almost a year since David and Tony had met and they had grown apart. Now there were some hard business facts to deal with if the Mainman plan for world domination

was going to be achieved. The facts read much like this: the US charts. 'Pin-Ups' (top 30), 'Aladdin Sane' (top 30), 'Hunky Dory' (top 100), 'Space Oddity' (top 30), 'Ziggy Stardust' (top 30), and 'The Man Who Sold The World' (top 100). Not bad but not fantastic. David had also never had a US Top 10 single. In other words, he was doing well but he wasn't really the superstar that De Fries was always telling RCA he was. The new album had to be promoted and that meant getting out on the road and selling it. 'The Last Concert' would be scrapped because it wasn't the last concert, there would be lots and lots more concerts.

Whether David liked this or not is hard to tell but he went along with it. Describing De Fries in an interview David said, 'We're very very strong buddies but I'm totally aware that if we had no business between us we'd never see each other. We're only buddies as long as we're in business together. He knows that as well I think.'

De Fries' attitude to David was just as straightforward. In a rare interview De Fries told Michael Watts how he visualised David.

'The way I think about David is as a building, because to me he represents potentially a building on Sixth Avenue, which I told him at a very early stage in our relationship. He has the potential — in my hands, anyway — to create the income to make a building on Sixth Avenue. In other words, he is the beginning, potentially, of an empire syndrome.'

For the time being, anyway, David continued to go along with it. He stayed in New York and began preparations for a mammoth tour of the States, the 'Diamond Dogs' tour. Preparations for the tour took two months during which time, apart from rehearsals, David absorbed some of the life of Manhattan. In an interview with Martin Kirkup in Sounds he told what he had been doing. 'Ever since I got to New York I've been going down to the Apollo in Harlem. Most New Yorkers seem scared to go there if they're white but the music's incredible. I saw The Temptations and the Spinners together on the same bill there and next week it's Marvin Gaye. Incredible! I love that kind of thing.

'I'm putting a very good new band together. There'll be three people from the 'Diamond Dogs' album, Mike Garson on piano again, Herbie Flowers on bass — I managed to persuade Herbie to tour with me, he's got to be the best bassist in the country, and there's Tony Newman who used to drum in the old Jeff Beck group. I've also been looking for guitars and I've found a really incredible black guy called Carlos. I want a really funky sound.'

The 'Diamond Dogs' tour opened on June 14 in Montreal. It was a 90 minute, 20 song show, completely choreographed and arranged and with dozens of carefully rehearsed special effects. The set was a disintegrating metropolis, Hunger City, composed of three lighting towers, constructed to look like the tops of skyscrapers, a tall phallic tower which dripped blood and a 20 foot high catwalk which rose and fell at David's command. To the horror of all the platform shod, spiky haired fans in the audience, David appeared in flat shoes and wearing a fluffy hair style with a parting.

Each song was linked to the next one and presented with theatrical effects beginning with '1984'. After 'Rebel, Rebel' and 'Moonage Daydream', David appeared on the catwalk for the first time while yellow lamp standards gave the set an eerie night-time glow and David strolled about in a long trench coat while dancers mimed the lyrics. The whole catwalk swung silently to the ground with David arriving just on the opening beat of 'Changes'. 'Suffragette City', 'All The Young Dudes' and 'Will You Rock And Roll With Me' ended the first act with David taking a

theatrical bow as the house lights went up.

The band stood to the side of the stage and were not allowed to intrude visually on what was happening. Earl Slick was on guitar plus Herbie Flowers on bass, Mike Garson on keyboards, and Tony Newman on drums. Dancers Warren Peace (from the Astronettes) and Gui Andrisan also sing backup and move the props and microphones around stage to avoid roadies having to appear. The whole set was created at enormous expense by set designer Jules Fisher who had previously done the award winning sets for 'Hair', 'Lenny', 'Pippin' and 'Ulysses In Nighttown'. Choreography was by Toni Basil.

Act 2 opened with 'Watch That Man' followed by 'Drive In Saturday' which was David's only acoustic number of the show. When Earl Slick hit the opening power chord of 'Space Oddity' David appeared to have left the stage, then a door at the top of one of the skyscrapers swung open to reveal David sitting on a seat at the end of a long hydraulic pole which extended out so that finally he was seated far above the heads of the front rows of the audience. The attention to detail was such that he sang 'Space Oddity' into a radio telephone apparatus instead of a conventional microphone. With multi-coloured lights flashing he assumed completely the identity of Major Tom.

The effects came thick and fast. During 'Diamond Dogs' he was tied with ropes by the dancers while for 'Panic In Detroit' a boxing ring appeared and David was wearing big red boxing gloves. There was even a big Black bodyguard to act as his second and change his gum shield between verses and towel him down.

The last half hour was even more bizarre. David appeared sitting on a platform of mirrors which he climbed inside. The dancers opened the doors and — just like a conjuring trick — there was no David, just a gigantic sparkling black hand lit by ultraviolet lamps. The hand lowered and became a glittering staircase for David to make another entrance on. The finale was 'The Jean Genie' and 'Rock And Roll Suicide' as a medley with small powerful spots throwing huge shadows of David and the dancers on the walls of the menacing skyscrapers. Suddenly it was over and David was gone. The audience cheered for ten minutes but to no avail. No encores, in fact he had already left the theatre.

The July 14 and 15 dates at Tower Theatre in Philadelphia were recorded for a live album though these were by no means the best gigs on the tour. The recording should probably have been made later in the tour when they had tightened up.

The 'Diamond Dogs' tour was a great success. It grossed over $5m though the original set by Jules Fisher cost $200,000. Now all David needed to do was crack the top ten with a really commercial single. While RCA busied themselves releasing the double album 'David Live' while the publicity was still hot, David moved into the elegant Hotel Barclay on Rittenhouse Square in Philadelphia. He had time booked at Sigma Sound studios, studios legendary for the R&B sound of Gamble and Huff.

He gathered together a formidable lineup: Carlos Alomar, and David Sanborne who had been on the 'Diamond Dogs' tour, the former playing guitar and the latter on alto sax and flute. Now David added Andy Newmark, a drummer from Sly and the Family Stone, and Willie Weeks, a bass player who had worked with, among others, Aretha Franklin. Both men were a little uncertain about working with Bowie as David explained, 'When Andy and Willie came to see me in the studio they were very wary. They didn't know what to expect. They came in looking for silver capes and all, I imagine. But once we started playing the songs it worked itself out. It

(PHOTO: L.F.I.)

'Diamond Dogs'
RCA APL 1 0576.   Released May 1974.
Producer: David Bowie.
Arranger: David Bowie, except track 9, Tony Visconti.
Studios: Olympic, Island, London, and Studio L. Ludolf, Hilversum, Holland.
Engineer: Keith Harwood.
1. **Future Legend** (Bowie)
2. **Diamond Dogs** (Bowie)
3. **Sweet Thing** (Bowie)
4. **Candidate** (Bowie)
5. **Sweet Thing (Reprise)** (Bowie)
6. **Rebel Rebel** (Bowie)
7. **Rock 'n' Roll With Me** (Words: Bowie. Music: Bowie, Peace)
8. **We Are The Dead** (Bowie)
9. **1984** (Bowie)
10. **Big Brother** (Bowie)
11. **Chant Of The Ever Circling Skeletal Family** (Bowie)
David Bowie: Vocals, guitar, saxophones, Mellotron, Moog synthesizer.
Tony Newman: Drums.

Aynsley Dunbar: Drums.
Herbie Flowers: Bass.
Mike Garson: Keyboards.
Alan Parker: Guitar on track 9.

Rebel Rebel (Bowie) / **Queen Bitch** (Bowie)
RCA LPBO 5009.   Released February 15, 1974.
Producers: Side A, David Bowie, for Mainman. Side B, Ken Scott, assisted by the actor, for Gem.
Arranger: David Bowie.
Side B taken from 'Hunky Dory'.

Rock 'n' Roll Suicide (Bowie) / **Quicksand** (Bowie)
RCA LPBO 5021.   Released April 11, 1974.
Producers: Side A, David Bowie, Ken Scott, for Mainman. Side B, Ken Scott, assisted by the actor, for Mainman.
Side A taken from 'The Rise And Fall Of Ziggy Stardust And The Spiders From Mars'.
Side B taken from 'Hunky Dory'.

ended in a very very solid friendship and a group that is going to work with me.'

David was very pleased with the album, so pleased in fact that he played it to journalist Robert Hilburn when instead he should have been giving him a preview of the 'David Live' album. 'We cut it in a week in Philadelphia and it can tell you more about where I am now than anything I could say.'

He described the making of the album, 'When we were recording a bunch of kids stayed outside the studio all night, until 10 o'clock in the morning, so we let them in and played some things from the album and they loved it, which was amazing. Fabulous, because I really didn't know what they'd think about the change in direction...

'It's just emotional drive. It's one of the first albums I've done that bounds along on emotional impact. There's not a concept in sight and that's where I felt my area as a writer was, but I've obviously changed. When I finished this album I felt, 'My God, I'm a different writer than I used to be'. Before you put it all together, you don't know what you've really got — just bits and pieces. But then, when we listened to it all together, it was obvious that I had really really changed. Far more than I had thought. Every time I play a finished album I get shock. I think, 'Wow, is that where I am now?'

The album was tentatively titled 'One Damn Song' but of course went on to become 'Young Americans'. Though everyone took it to be a totally new departure, David saw it very much as an extension of 'Diamond Dogs'. 'Diamond Dogs' was the start of this album. Things like 'Rock and Roll With Me' and '1984' were embryonic of what I wanted to do. I tried all kinds of things. It was not a concept album. It was a collection of things. And I didn't have a band so that's where the tension came in. I couldn't believe I had finished it when I did. I had done so much of it myself. I never want to be in that position again. It was frightening trying to make an album with no support behind you. I was very much on my own. It was my more difficult album. It was a relief that it did so well.

'Even then, the songs on 'Diamond Dogs' that I got the biggest kick out of — like 'Rock and Roll With Me' and '1984' — gave me the knowledge that there was another album at least inside of me that I was going to be happy with. I mean, if I can't make albums that I'm happy with, I'll not make them. I won't just go in and knock off dozens of albums. They must mean something to me. It just happens that I write very fast. That's why I seem to have so many bloody albums out.'

September found David living in Los Angeles and planning yet another tour. The first thing he had to do was terminate his elaborate stage show. The next tour was to be very straight. 'I think I always know when to stop doing something. It's when the enjoyment is gone. That's why I've changed so much. I've never been of the opinion that it's necessarily a wise thing to keep on a successful streak if you're just duplicating all the time.

'I have now done what I wanted to do three or four years ago — stage an elaborate, colourful show — a fantasy, and I don't think I want to go any further with it because I know it can be done. I know I could do an even bigger, grander kind of production. But when I know it can be done, I don't have to do it anymore.

'Doing a straight show is very exciting to me now; suddenly jumping into a new kind of tour after this one. I couldn't imagine just doing the same show over and over again. It would be terribly boring. That's why I gave up the last time. That's why I 'retired' last time.'

DAVID LIVE

'David Live'
RCA APL2 0771. Released October 1974.
Producer: Tony Visconti.
Studio: Recorded live at the Tower Theatre, Philadelphia, Pa., July 12-13, 1974, by Keith Harwood.
Mixed by Tony Visconti, Edwin H. Kramer, at Electric Ladyland, New York.
1. **1984** (Bowie)
2. **Rebel, Rebel** (Bowie)
3. **Moonage Daydream** (Bowie)
4. **Sweet Thing** (Bowie)
5. **Changes** (Bowie)
6. **Suffragette City** (Bowie)
7. **Aladdin Sane** (Bowie)
8. **All the Young Dudes** (Bowie)
9. **Cracked Actor** (Bowie)
10. **When You Rock 'n' Roll With Me** (Bowie, Peace)
11. **Watch That Man** (Bowie)
12. **Knock On Wood** (Floyd, Cropper)
13. **Diamond Dogs** (Bowie)
14. **Big Brother** (Bowie)
15. **Width Of A Circle** (Bowie)
16. **Jean Genie** (Bowie)
17. **Rock 'n' Roll Suicide** (Bowie)

Diamond Dogs (Bowie) / **Holy Holy** (Bowie)
RCA APBO 0293. Released June 14, 1974.
Producers: Side A, David Bowie for Mainman.
Side B, David Bowie, Ken Scott for Mainman.
Side A taken from the album 'Diamond Dogs'.
Side B is a re-issue of the single from 1971.

Knock On Wood (Floyd, Cropper) / **Panic In Detroit** (Bowie)
RCA 2456. Released September 13, 1974.
Producer: Tony Visconti for Mainman.

David was spending all of his time in the USA now and was reported as having bought a house in Geneva, just outside Los Angeles where he spent his time assembling a library of 30,000 books. Other reports suggest that his period in Los Angeles was more self-destructive than self-improving. Certainly the interviews he gave later always described L.A. as such.

'Young Americans', the single, came out on February 21st with the US pressing having a different mix and being almost two minutes shorter. It was followed a few weeks later by the album. It was the second single from the album which really tipped the scales. 'Fame', co-written and co-performed with John Lennon, gave David his first US number one.

As the album and the single climbed the charts, David began the complicated procedure of separating himself from Tony De Fries and the Mainman organisation. Lawsuits flew and were met by counter-suits. De Fries saw his skyscraper on Sixth Avenue disappearing over the horizon and fought hard to keep it. He knew that without Bowie he was no-one. David pressed on and finally extricated himself commenting, 'The dispute had been building up for some time. I guess it was a bit hard for them to come to terms with what I wanted to do. A lot of people who I never even met got involved. I grew to dislike their attitude so I just said 'Goodbye'. David set up his own company, Bewlay Brothers, to look after his affairs and began thinking about film and television exposure.

David's stay in Los Angeles produced many weird rumours one among them being that he was engaged in a study of witchcraft and actively drawing pentagrams and muttering spells, but then Satanism was very big in Hollywood that year ... In a doom laden telephone interview with Ram Magazine he prophesied a grim future, 'Dictatorship. There will be a political figure in the not too distant future who'll sweep this part of world like rock 'n' roll did. You probably hope that I'm not right but I am. My predictions are very accurate, always.'

David moved to New York and settled in the Chelsea district just north of Greenwich Village. It was here that he became involved in the film 'The Man Who Fell To Earth'. David described what happened in Cream Magazine.

'They were first thinking of using Peter O'Toole for the part. Then Nick happened to see me in a documentary ('Cracked Actor') that the BBC aired on a show called Omnibus and thought I might be good for the role. I was in New York at the time and he flew in to see me. I was really terrible. I kept him waiting eight hours. I was out and when I remembered the appointment I was already an hour late, so I thought, 'Oh no, I missed him, he won't be there now', and just forgot about it. When I finally got home, there was Nick waiting for me, sitting in my kitchen very patiently. Eight hours late and the man waited for me! That's persistence you know, isn't it? So we sat in the kitchen talking about the film and different things for hours and by the time he left I'd decided to do the film.'

After some script changes David signed the contract and prepared for the shooting which was to begin that summer in New Mexico.

David arrived in New Mexico on board the famous Santa Fe Super Chief bringing with him a personal library of over 1500 books as well as the contents of his art studio. 'I take everything with me I would normally have at home. That's one of the benefits of travelling by train — you can fill up all the compartments as there are usually so few other people travelling.'

Apart from a lot of reading and painting in between takes, David also worked on preparing a book of short stories called 'The Return Of The Thin White Duke' which he described at the time as 'partly autobiographical, mostly fiction, with a deal of magic in it.' On one of his days off from

1975

shooting he visited a Tibetan monastery in nearby Taos where the chief Lama was an old friend of his. With him he took a record player specially adapted to play records backwards because David had discovered that 'Young Americans' played backwards sounded uncannily like a Tibetan chant.

With David in New Mexico were Angie and four year old Zowie. David had long been fascinated by movies and was immediately drawn to Nick Roeg, 'It didn't take me long to realise the man was a genius'. In an interview with Cream Magazine on the set he said, 'Working with Nick is nice because we get on well, we understand one another. There's a marvellous chemistry between us. He's very sensitive to everything that's going on. He's brilliant.' It was a mutual admiration society with Roeg saying more or less the same about David, 'David is a true Renaissance man. His qualities are absolute. He is like no other person I have ever met.'

In addition to acting in 'The Man Who Fell To Earth' David was supposed to write the soundtrack music. He announced it as his next album, planned for a March 1976 release, and after filming he left for New York to write it but it was not to be.

The litigation was still in progress against De Fries and this may have had something to do with the soundtrack's non appearance. There is no doubt that one was planned and the movie even features a hit album (which in the event, we never got to hear). How much of the movie soundtrack was finally used on the next album 'Station to Station' is hard to say. David uses a still from the movie on the sleeve.

Back in New York David got together 'Young American' veterans Dennis Davis, Carlos Alomar and Earl Slick. He recruited Bruce Springsteen's pianist Roy Battin and bass player George Murray and flew the lot of them to Los Angeles where he had time booked at Cherokee studios. David of course travelling by train, in fact the album opens with the chuffing of a train.

Harry Masslin, who took over from Tony Visconti on 'Young Americans' co-produced with David. The album took two and a half months to record with final mastering taking place in mid December. It was recorded in 24 track and posed a fair number of problems because, though the band could rehearse the songs, David often makes substantial changes while recording. Most of it was therefore improvised.

While in Los Angeles, David made a rare public appearance by making his US TV debut in an unannounced performance on Cher's weekly TV show. 'I adored working with him and was delighted to have him on the show' said Cher, somewhat predictably.

With 'Fame' in the number one spot in the US charts for four weeks David was in a position to do anything he wanted. He obviously thought the MOR audience needed to see him. The show was taped in mid October for November 9th transmission and David sang 'Fame' to a backing track while Cher joined him to duet on 'Can You Hear Me' from 'Young Americans'. The performance included an absurd tongue in cheek medley opening with 'Young Americans' then Neil Diamond's 'Song Sung Blue'. Harry Nilsson's 'One' was followed by Phil Spector's classic 'Da Doo Ron Ron' which was Cher's first ever recording when she sang along in the chorus on The Ronettes original version. In the chorus this time was Spector artist Darlene Love. The duet continued through 'Wedding Bell Blues', 'Maybe' and 'Day Tripper'. Bill Withers' 'Ain't No Sunshine' led to The Coasters' 'Youngblood' and then back at the start again with 'Young Americans'.

On the set with David was his lawyer Michael Lippman who announced the lawsuit with De Fries was settled. 'This won't be a situation like the Stones where the market will be flooded with

DAVID FILMING 'THE MAN WHO FELL TO EARTH'.

DAVID, ANGIE AND ZOWIE (PHOTO: REX FEATURES)

Young Americans (Bowie) / **Suffragette City** (Bowie)
RCA 2523.   Released February 21, 1975.
Producer: Tony Visconti.
Arranger: Side A, David Bowie.
The US pressing of the single was a different mix and almost 2 minutes shorter: 3m 11s instead of 5m 01s.
Side B is taken from the 'David Live' album.

London Boys (Bowie) / **Love You Till Tuesday** (Bowie)
Decca F 13579.   Released May 1975.
Producer: Mike Vernon.
Musical director: Side B, Dek Fearnley.
Re-issue of 1966 and 1967 material from Decca.
Side A from 1966 single. Side B from 1967 album 'Love You Till Tuesday'.

'Young Americans'

RCA RS 1006.   Released March 1975.
Producers: Track 1, Tony Visconti. Tracks 2-5,
Tony Visconti, Harry Maslin. Tracks 6-8, David
Bowie, Harry Maslin.
Studios: Tracks 1-5, 7, Sigma Sound,
Philadelphia. Tracks 6,8, Electric Lady, New
York. Track 1 mixed at Sound House, London.
Tracks 2-8 mixed at Record Plant, New York.
Engineers: Sigma Sound, Carl Parulow. Elec-
tric Lady, Eddie Kramer. Record Plant, Harry
Maslin.
Arrangers: String arrangements - Tony Viscon-
ti. Vocal arrangements - David Bowie, Luther
Vandross.

1. **Young Americans** (Bowie)
2. **Win** (Bowie)
3. **Fascination** (Words: Bowie, Vandross.
   Music: Vandross)
4. **Right** (Bowie)
5. **Somebody Up There Likes Me** (Bowie)
6. **Across The Universe** (Lennon, McCartney)
7. **Can You Hear Me** (Bowie)

David Bowie: Vocals, guitar, keyboards, v
back-up.
Carlos Alomar: Guitar.
Earl Slick: Guitar.
Dennis Davis: Drums.
Andy Newmark: Drums.
Emir Ksasan: Bass.
Willy Weeks: Bass.
John Lennon: Guitar on tracks 6 and 8. Ba
up vocals on track 8.
Michael Garson: Keyboards.
David Sanborn: Saxophone.
Ralph McDonald: Percussion.
Pable Rosario: Percussion.
Larry Washington: Percussion.
Ava Cherry: Back-up vocal.
Robin Clark: Back-up vocal.
Jean Fineberg: Back-up vocal on track 8.
Anthony Hinton: Back-up vocal on track 8.
Jean Millington: Back-up vocal on track 8.
Warren Peace: Back-up vocal.
Diane Sumler: Back-up vocal.
Luther Vandross: Back-up vocal.

'Images'
Deram DPA 3017/8.   Released May 1975.
Producers: Mike Vernon, except track 21, Tony Visconti.
Musical directors: tracks 2,3,5,8 - 17,19,20, Dek Fearnley. Track 4, Ivor Raymonde.
1. **Rubber Band** (Bowie)
2. **Maid of Bond Street** (Bowie)
3. **Sell Me A Coat** (Bowie)
4. **Love You Till Tuesday** (Bowie)
5. **There Is A Happy Land** (Where Only Children Go) (Bowie)
6. **The Laughing Gnome** (Bowie)

17. **Please Mr. Gravedigger** (Bowie)
18. **London Boys** (Bowie)
19. **Karma Man** (Bowie)
20. **Let Me Sleep Beside You** (Bowie)
21. **In The Heat Of The Morning** (Bowie)
A compilation of everything issued by Der
'Love You Till Tuesday' album plus the fou
tracks added on 'The World of David Bowi
and the single 'The Laughing Gnome' / 'Th
Gospel According To Tony Day'.

DAVID BOWIE

FAME RIGHT

Fame (Bowie, Lennon, Alomar) / **Right** (Bowie)
RCA 2579.   Released August 18, 1975.
Producers: Side A, David Bowie, Harry Maslin
Side B, Tony Visconti.
Taken from 'Young Americans' album.

Space Oddity (Bowie) / **Changes** (Bowie),
Velvet Goldmine (Bowie)
RCA 2593.   Released September 26, 1975.
Producers: Side A, Gus Dudgeon. Side B, Ken
Scott assisted by The Actor.
Issued as part of RCA's 'Maximillion' series of
three tracks for the price of two re-issues. The

greatest hits repackages. All product must have David's consent' Lippman told Harvey Kubernik. David had decided to use TV and films to reach the public and saw no need to tour, 'There are very few who have broken out of rock and into any other medium, much less films. I'm determined to do it. The media should be used. You can't let it use you, which is what is happening to the majority of rock stars around. As for touring, I honestly believe that it kills my art. I will never ever tour again.' However, a short time later David had to announce a 35 city US tour. 'It will make me an obscenely large amount of money' he explained. He needed capital for his film production company Bewlay Bros Inc.

Without lifting a finger he was making money back in the UK. RCA's re-issue of 'Space Oddity' had reached number one in the charts, six years after it was first released. It had been about two years since David was in Britain. David finished off 1975 by appearing on the normally all Black programme 'Soul Train' in the States and singing his new single, 'Golden Years'. Though he later admitted that he had to get drunk to do it, he was rewarded with seeing the record climb the R&B charts as well as the Top 100.

91

In early December Londoners had a chance to see David on television when he appeared in a satellite interview with Russell Harty on LWTV. David doing his part from TV studios in Burbank, Los Angeles. It was 3am for David and 11am for Russell. The interview remained on a mundane level throughout but David did announce a European tour and that he was setting up house in Switzerland for Angie and Zowie to live in during the tour.

The tour which David announced on the Russell Harty show was his first live appearance in the US since the Spring 1974 'Young Americans' tour. The 35 city North American segment began on February 2nd in Vancouver, B.C. ended on March 26 at Madison Square Garden, New York City. That was followed by David's first concert tour of Europe and concerts in Britain.

Tens of thousands of fans arrived dressed in glitter and weird makeup, expecting the same kind of extravagant spectacle as the previous tours had been. From the very beginning they realised that this time it would be different because the show opened with Salvador Dali and Luis Bunuel's surrealist movie 'Un Chien Andalou' which few of the glitter freaks understood. Then on strolled David, very casual in plain white shirt, black waistcoat and trousers. His hair was still a reddish blonde but was cut short and swept back. He crooned his way through his songs, very elegantly, smoking an endless chain of Gitanes. Behind him were a tough funky rhythm section composed of Carlos Alomar, guitar, who worked on 'Station To Station', Stacey Haydon, guitar, brought in to replace Earl Slick who pulled out at the last minute in the company of David's short lived manager Michael Lippman. George Murray on bass and Dennis Davis on drums were both from the 'Station To Station' sessions. Tony Kaye on keyboards was another last minute addition. 'There are three blacks and three whites, including myself, and that's a good mixture' commented David in an interview with Chris Charlesworth.

Earl Slick withdrew at the last moment because he made a number of unacceptable demands in order to go on the road. Slick demanded to be brought up front on stage, get more press, more pay and also pay for the other three members of the Earl Slick band who wouldn't be able to work while their leader was on tour. Since it was obvious that not one person was buying their ticket to see Slick there seemed little point in continuing. Slick left to start a solo career, getting initial publicity on the way by being as unpleasant as possible about Bowie and the 'Young Americans' album, 'It's the most boring thing I've ever played on. In fact it's the most boring thing I've ever heard.' The public seemed to feel the same way about Slick's own album when it finally appeared.

The set was very simply lit with pure white light designed by tour manager Eric Barrett. 'It's more theatrical than 'Diamond Dogs' ever was. It's by suggestion rather than over-propping. It relies on modern 20th century theatre concepts of lighting and I think it comes over as being very theatrical. Whether the audiences are aware of it I don't know.'

'I wanted to use a new kind of staging and I think this staging will become one of the most important ever. It will affect every kind of rock and roll act from now on because it's the most stabilised move that I've seen in rock and roll. I've reverted to pure Brechtian theatre and I've never seen Brechtian theatre used like this since Morrison and The Doors and even then Morrison never used white light like I do.'

The concerts were quite a shock to the Ziggy lookalike kids but David soon pulled them in. David regarded it as a bit of a joke. He told Bob Hart 'It's a bit naughty I suppose but I love to tease them. I don't want anybody to take me for granted. It was a carefully calculated effect. No makeup except for a touch around the eyes. Stark white light just like they used in the German theatre in the 30s and no props, unless you count my cigarettes.

'There was a real danger that one day there would be so many things on stage that I would disappear completely. So I have gone to the other extreme. It seems to work and it allows me to enjoy my music and my band more than ever before.'

In the Charlesworth interview he explained what was wrong with the 'Diamond Dogs' show. 'It was just boring after a while. Once I got to Los Angeles and did the shows in the Amphitheatre

1976

here I'd already done thirty of them and it was terrible. There's nothing more boring than a stylised show because there was no spontaneity and no freedom of movement. Everything was totally choreographed and it was very stiff. It didn't look it if you went and saw the show once. The first time it was probably a gas but there's nothing much in it if you are doing it every night. It just becomes repetition.

'This one changes almost every night. It's a lot looser. The only thing we have is a running order but I even change that around. The lighting guys have lighting cues but that's on spec as well.'

The show concentrated on numbers from 'Station to Station' and 'Young Americans', both albums which required a tight rhythm section. The show opened with 'Station To Station' moved through 'Suffragette City', 'Word On A Wing', 'TVC 15' which was one of the numbers written for 'The Man Who Fell To Earth' movie before being included on 'Station To Station' and 'Panic In Detroit' on which he played a little saxophone. 'Rebel Rebel' was used as an encore.

There was another big difference between the 'Station To Station' tour and the 'Diamond Dogs' tour. He actually made some money. 'I never saw any money from the 'Diamond Dogs' tour. I'm only making money now. That's why I wanted to simplify things this time around, to make money. I'm managing myself now, simply because I've got fed up with managers I've known.'

Gone were the enormous entourage. David now honed his staff down to three people. Pat Gibbons as acting manager, Corinne Schwab, secretary and Barbara De Witt to handle press relations. 'My office is a suitcase that stays in my room. It's far better than before when I never knew what was going on and this is how I used to do it back in England before.'

He described the situation on other tours, 'The other tours were misery, so painful. I had amazing amounts of people on the road with me. I had a management system that had no idea what it was doing and was totally self-interested and pompous. They never dealt with the people on the road so I was getting all those problems. Every night ten or fifteen people would be coming to see me and laying their problems on me because the management couldn't or wouldn't deal with it. For me, touring was no fun, no fun at all. The two major tours I did were horrendous experiences. I hated every minute of them so I used to say I'd never tour again, then I'd be talked into doing it again to make somebody some money.

'This time though I will be touring again. We've got it down to a sensible number and it works. It's the most efficient tour I've ever been on. Everybody on this tour is in a wonderful mood. This time no-one comes to me with problems so we get together as people instead and I actually find I'm spending time with the band which is rare. I have actually written on the road this time. I've never been able to do that before.'

The tour was a great success, particularly the taking of San Francisco by storm. When David played The Winterland Auditorium during the Ziggy tour of 1972 only 1,100 people turned up to see him in the 5,000 seater stadium. The turnout was so disappointing that he gave San Francisco a miss during the next tour. But this time round, helped by his number one single 'Fame', he sold out San Francisco's biggest auditorium, the 14,000 seater Cow Palace. What is more, the audience kept shouting and clapping long after the house lights had been turned on after the encore and David had to do an unprepared second encore — a hastily assembled version of 'Diamond Dogs' in which he fluffed some of the words. Even after this, with the house lights on again the audience cheered for a full five minutes more. It was the strongest response to a concert at the Cow Palace in years.

The only little hiccup on the whole tour seemed to be a small matter of a pot bust during the East Coast leg. The New York Post of March 22, 1976 reported: 'Bowie plus three companions ordered to appear in court in Rochester, NY, on Thursday to answer marijuana charges. Arrested at the Flagship Americana Hotel, Rochester, police found 8oz of marijuana and charged them with criminal possession. James Ousterberg and Duane Vaughns, both of 224 Jefferson Ave, Brooklyn left Rochester last night for Springfield, Mass., for a concert. They were to go from there to New Haven. Bowie put up bail for all four persons of $2,000 each. The woman, Chiwah Soo, 20, of Rochester did not travel on. State police said that the hotel had been under surveillance for several hours.'

In the Charlesworth interview David explained in detail his thoughts about his career. 'I just do anything as it comes up. I've learned to find a much calmer level of intensity these days. I don't push for much but I seem to move a lot faster when I do things this way. I think I've done the bit that I needed to do in rock and roll. I've made my contribution to rock and roll and the only thing I can do now, if I stay in rock and roll, is to have a rock and roll career. Not being very career minded, I don't want a career in rock and roll.

'I don't believe it's possible for an artist to say more than two new things in rock and roll. One artist has one thing to say and it's such an ephemeral sort of culture that after he's said it, it's just a question of staying around. If you do strive to say something new, it gets interpreted as just another way of staying around.

' 'Fame' kind of put a cap on things. It told me I could finish now, pack it all in now. That meant I had done the two things I was supposed to do, which is to conquer this market and conquer the British market. Once you have done that you can pretend to rest on your laurels and all the other cliches you can do when you hit the top. You can forget longevity and all the things that make you stay there as far as I'm concerned. All that staying at the top is just a heartache for me. I just want to do what I want to do, and first that is make some money with this tour and enjoy making it at the same time.'

'I've been trained in a career as a rock and roll singer and I now see that I do that very well. Therefore like any good chap who has a career, I should utilise my talents and the training that I've got and make some money out of it. You have to own up to that after a while. I'm enjoying this tour so I'll do some more tours.

'Albums? I'll make some commercial albums and I'll make some albums that possibly aren't as commercial. I'll probably keep alternating, providing myself with a hit album to make the money to do the next album which probably won't sell as well.'

At this point, in March 1976, David revealed that he had recorded an electronic album 'without vocals that you'd recognise' and he had been talking for a while about Brian Eno and Kraftwerk. The new direction that his music was to take was already clear to him, even though he was still in the middle of a funky disco tour.

In late February David interrupted his tour to appear on the Dinah Shore show, the Hollywood showbiz chat show. The show was co-hosted by Nancy Walker and 'Fonzie' Henry Winkler. David sang 'Stay' and 'Five Years'. He showed his mastery of the television medium during the chat. Dinah Shore: 'Rock and roll has been very good to you.' David: 'I've been very good for rock and roll'.

David arrived in Britain in May after a three year absence and proceeded to play six nights at

(PHOTO: MICHAEL PUTLAND, L.F.I.)

STATIONTOSTATIONDAVIDBOWIE

'Station To Station'
RCA APLI 1327.   Released January 1976.
Producers: David Bowie, Harry Maslin.
Arranged by David Bowie.
1. **Station To Station** (Bowie)
2. **Golden Years** (Bowie)
3. **Word On A Wing** (Bowie)
4. **TVC 15** (Bowie)
5. **Stay** (Bowie)
6. **Wild Is The Wind** (Tiomkin)
Carlos Alomar: Guitar.
Roy Bittan: Piano.
Dennis Davis: Drums.
George Murray: Bass.
Warren Peace: Back-up vocal.
Earl Slick: Guitar.

TVC 15 (Bowie) / **We Are The Dead** (Bowie)
RCA 2682.   Released April 30, 1976.
Producers: Side A, David Bowie, Harry Maslin.
Side B, David Bowie for Mainman.
Arranger: Side A, David Bowie.
Side A taken from 'Station To Station'.
Side B taken from 'Diamond Dogs'.

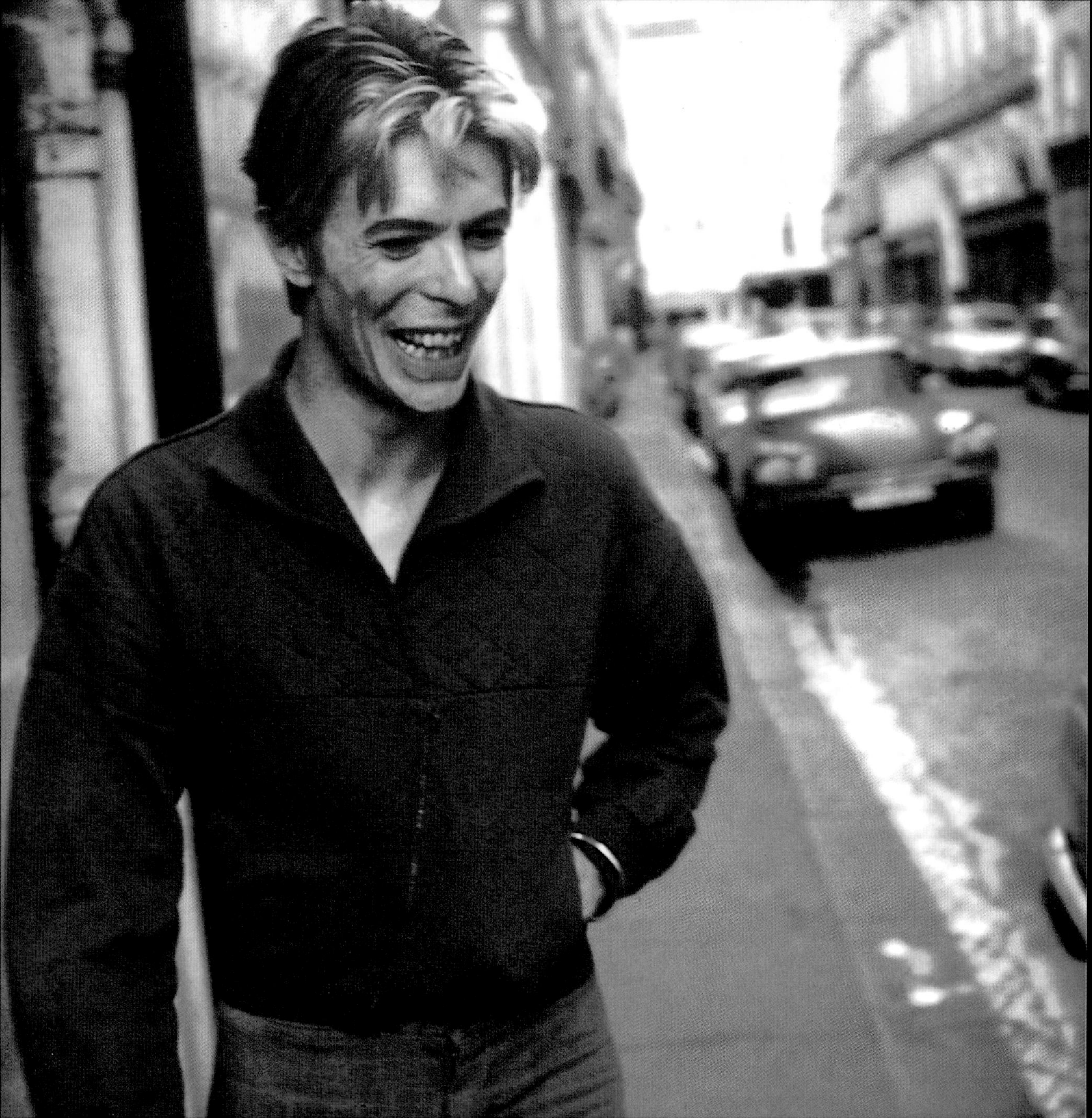

(PHOTO: L.F.I.

Wembley before an audience of close on 60,000 people. He played the same set as the American concerts, strangely not even doing the title track from 'Young Americans'. In fact 'Fame' was the only 'Young Americans' track on the song list. The omission of 'Space Oddity' was good and finally brought his repertoire up to date. Many of the fans arrived in up to date Bowie outfits, having seen the photographs of the white shirt and black waistcoat in the music papers. David stuck with the image. It was an emotional return for some and after the final encore of 'The Jean Genie' on the first night, there were tears in David's eyes at the reception his English fans gave him after so many years.

He travelled on to Switzerland where he was setting up house for Angela and Zowie and where Zowie was going to attend school.

He moved into the Chateau d'Herouville, where he had made 'Pin Ups' and began work on producing 'The Idiot' for Iggy Pop. David had previously mixed the tapes of 'Raw Power' back in 1973 at Western Sound in Hollywood and at the same time introduced Iggy to the Mainman organisation. Iggy had become a very close friend of David and was travelling with him on the 'Station To Station' tour. He was one of the people arrested for pot in Rochester, NY. With the collapse of Mainman David took over as Iggy's manager.

This was a bad period for David. The new owners of the Chateau had let it deteriorate. The engineers were useless and David and Tony Visconti both came down with dysentery which put them to bed for two days. One of the reasons he chose the Chateau was to get away from all the hangers on from the States but they found out where he was and began arriving. He also was involved in litigation with his previous manager Michael Lippman and had to spend a number of days in Paris in order to dissolve their relationship. Bowie was charging that, among other things, Lippman had pledged that Bowie would get the right to score 'The Man Who Fell To Earth' whereas John Phillips eventually got the job leaving David with a completed soundtrack album that he had made with Paul Buckmaster (who originally arranged 'Space Oddity' for him back in 1967.) Some of the unused material eventually showed up on other albums: 'TVC 15' was on 'Station To Station' and 'Subterraneans' appeared as the last track on 'Low'. After the four days in Paris he was feeling very low, hence the album title. There were few lyrics because David had nothing to say.

David tried to persuade Tony Visconti to produce Iggy's album for him but Visconti was too busy except to mix it later in Berlin. The album 'The Idiot' almost counts as a new Bowie album since all the numbers were co-written with Bowie except 'Calling Sister Midnight' which was a Bowie-Iggy-Carlos Alomar composition. Coming as it did, in 1977, the album didn't really make the impact that it should because the British press was all involved with the punk explosion. 'The Idiot' was one of the most powerful albums of the year. David called it 'The Idiot' after a painting he found dating from 1906 which bears a striking resemblance to Iggy.

The album David recorded next was the controversial 'Low' which the critics didn't know how to approach. The phoneticism instead of real words and the long mood pieces initially made RCA, David's record company, think that they'd been given another 'Metal Machine Music', the bizarre electronic album that Lou Reed gave them after a string of normal vocal albums. Though 'Low' was handed in by the November 16th deadline for Christmas release, RCA dithered about with it and finally scheduled it for 1977.

'Low' was important for another reason. It was David's first collaboration with Brian Eno. Eno was considerably surprised when he met David, to find that both David and Iggy could hum, note

'Changes onebowie'

RCA RS 1055.   Released May 1976.
Producers: Track 1, Gus Dudgeon. Tracks 2, 7 and 8, David Bowie for Mainman. Track 3, Ken Scott (assisted by the actor) for Gem. Tracks 4 and 5, Ken Scott and David Bowie for Gem. Track 6, Ken Scott and David Bowie for Mainman. Tracks 7 and 8, David Bowie for Mainman. Track 9, Tony Visconti. Tracks 10 and 11, David Bowie and Harry Maslin.
Arrangers: Track 1, David Bowie and Paul Buckmaster. Track 6, David Bowie and Mick Ronson. Tracks 2-5, 7-11, David Bowie.

1. **Space Oddity** (Bowie)
2. **John, I'm Only Dancing** (Bowie)
3. **Changes** (Bowie)
4. **Ziggy Stardust** (Bowie)
5. **Suffragette City** (Bowie)
6. **The Jean Genie** (Bowie)
7. **Diamond Dogs** (Bowie)
8. **Rebel Rebel** (Bowie)
9. **Young Americans** (Bowie)
10. **Fame** (Bowie)
11. **Golden Years** (Bowie, Lennon, Alomar)

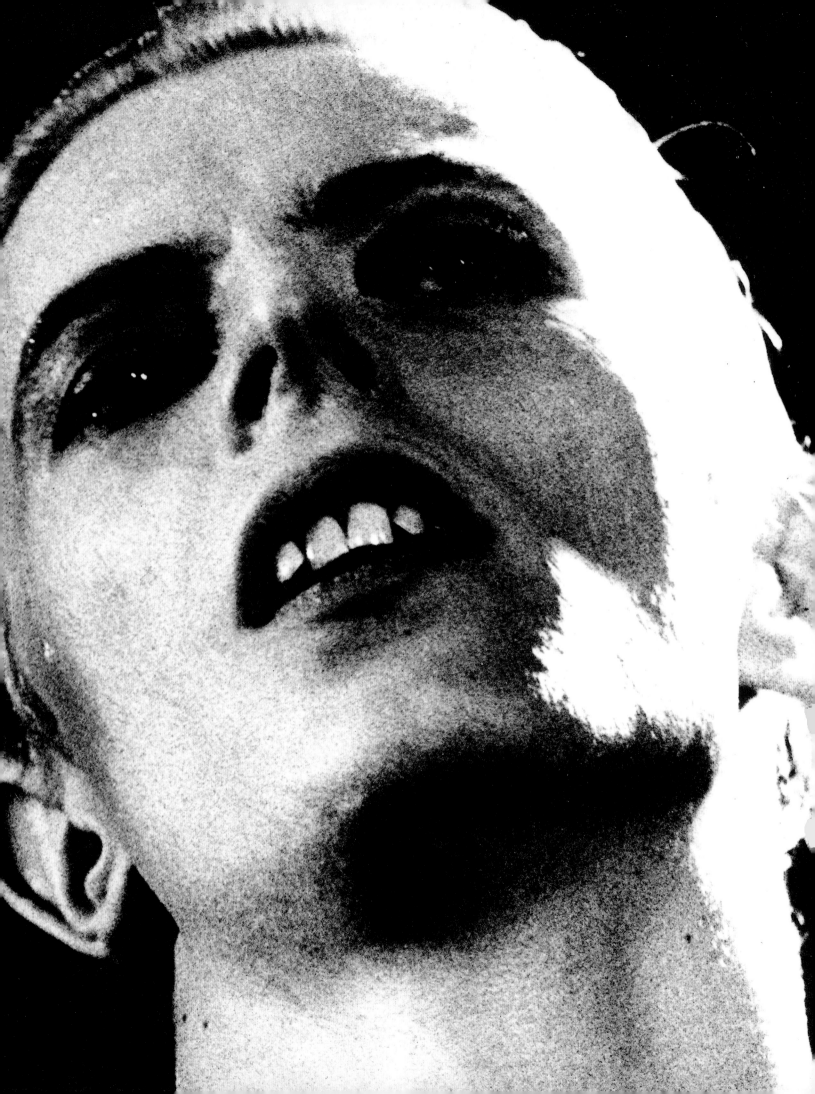

for note, the 'No Pussyfooting' album that he made with Robert Fripp. In an interview with the author for New Musical Express, Eno described what it was like working with David: 'We worked very well together, actually. There was a lucky break that took place. Well, first of all, we both work in very different ways: David works very fast. He's very impulsive and he works like crazy for about two hours or sometimes three-quarters of an hour — and then he takes the rest of the day off. And in that time, he does an incredible amount, very well, very quickly and faultlessly. He just puts on track after track and they're all just right and then he goes away, and that's it for the day. Quite often that's how it works.

'Whereas what I do is to — quite slowly — build things up over a period, you know. Since I'm using a monophonic synthesizer, it's incredibly tedious putting on one line at a time, "da-da-da-da..." like that. Very slow. So I got terribly nervous about working with other people around because so little seems to be happening.

'It's a very slow way of working, particularly with David who works quite the opposite, and the other thing of course: I keep taking things off and putting something else on instead — or I put on six tracks and take away the first three and that sort of thing. So I like to work alone really.

'Well, as it happened there were two days when we were at the Chateau Herouville — being at the Chateau meant that we had it booked all the time, you see — there were two days when David had to go to Paris to attend this court case or something like that — and the studio was still booked and it was still there so I said, 'Well, how about if I get on? I'll carry on working and I'll do some things and if you like them, we'll use them, and if you don't I'll use them myself, see, which struck me as an ideal deal. That meant that I could work without any guilty conscience about wasting someone else's time. Because if he hadn't wanted to use them, I would have paid him for the studio time and used them on my own album.

'Well, as it happened, I did a couple of things that I thought were very very nice and he liked a lot. One of them's a long piece, about six-and-a-half minutes long, and it's a very long, grave, solemn instrumental thing. David came in and put all the voices on it in about twenty minutes. There's about 110 voices on it!

'That was a perfect collaboration, you know. It was just right because I had all the time I needed to do this very tedious job of building up quite a big sounding thing from single notes and it was all there for him to come and work as fast as he wanted to on top of it. So that worked well.

'All the instrumentals on that track are by me and all the vocals are by him, so it's like I wrote and played all the music and he wrote and sang all the vocals.'

Brian Eno was at the Chateau for a week in September then David and Tony Visconti left for Berlin to complete both 'Low' and Iggy's 'The Idiot'. Berlin was to become David's home for most of 1977.

Berlin continued to fascinate David and he took a small apartment there over a car spares shop. He bought and cooked his own food, cleaned his own flat, grew a burgomaster's curling moustache, bought a flat cap and took to bicycling around town. 'I became a person again', he explained.

David's period in Los Angeles had done a lot of damage to him. 'I had a more than platonic relationship with drugs. Actually I was zonked out of my mind most of the time. You can do good things with drugs but then comes the long decline. I was skeletal. I was destroying my body' he told Rolling Stone. 'I was surrounded with people who indulged my ego, who treated me as Ziggy Stardust or one of my other characters, never realising that David Jones might be behind it.' In an interview in NME he put it more plainly, 'It's the most vile piss-pot in the world'.

David accomplished a lot in 1977. He recorded 'Heroes', another Iggy Pop album, 'Lust For Life', read 'Peter And The Wolf' for a spoken word album, spent time in Kenya and Switzerland and landed the leading role in the movie 'Just A Gigolo'.

The new Iggy album was a great achievement. Carlos Alomar and Ricky Gardiner played guitars, David played piano while the Sales brothers, Hunt and Tony played drums and bass respectively. The whole thing was done at the Hansa Tonstudios, 'Hansa by the Wall' in Berlin where 'Low' had been completed. In addition to producing the album, David co-wrote six of the songs with Iggy: Iggy writing the words, David providing the music.

Iggy went out on the road in March and David accompanied him on the gigs as his piano player. They played the UK and the States. There was a minor riot in New York during the concert at the Palladium in March. David remained at the piano, chainsmoking like a pub pianist and smiling contentedly.

David finished his new album 'Heroes' by mid-September. It was mostly recorded at Hansa though some parts were done at Mountain Studios, in Montreux, Switzerland where Angela and Zowie lived. 'Heroes' used his favourite line-up of Carlos Alomar on rhythm guitar, Dennis Davis on percussion, George Murray on bass, Brian Eno on synthesizers and keyboards and added a new face to the line-up, Robert Fripp on lead guitar. Fripp was just what David needed, his years with King Crimson proved he could play heavy rock riffs with the best of them but his 'No Pussyfooting' album with Eno and his later 'Frippertronics' showed he was up for some experimentation.

'Heroes' itself, written about two lovers who met each day in the shadow of the Berlin Wall just outside the studio, was recorded in English, French and German versions — a tribute to David's newly re-discovered 'European man'. Once the album was finished he returned to Angela in Switzerland. In an interview given that September he described Berlin, 'Berlin makes me feel uneasy, very claustrophobic. I work best under these sort of conditions. But I'm living in Switzerland right now. It's okay if you've got something specific to do, and I have, but I can understand people getting very bored over there.'

His next project was a TV show with his old friend Marc Bolan. The show was recorded at the Granada Studios in Manchester and also on the bill were Generation X and Eddie and the Hot Rods. David sang 'Heroes' and did a duet with Marc, backed by Herbie Flowers, Dino Dines and Tony Newman. Because the union insisted on blacking out at 7pm David and Marc never got beyond a rehearsal take, which they eventually used, and the Hot Rods never got to play at all despite waiting around in Manchester for two days.

On the train back to London David told the Rods that he had recorded a Christmas show with

1977

Bing Crosby. David always liked to surprise people. The show went out on September 28th.

Back in Montreux the next stage of David's career was taking shape. His Italian agent also acted for the actress Sydne Rome who had just been cast as the gigolo's childhood sweetheart in David Hemmings' up-coming movie 'Just a Gigolo'. David was suggested as the lead and Hemmings flew to Montreux to see him. He got the part. He arranged to return to Berlin for the winter for filming and in the meantime took a holiday in Kenya. He stayed in Mombasa and also at Treetops, the famous safari home of the British royal family. He did a lot of big game photography and managed to visit the Masai tribesmen. While in Berlin David began seriously painting again. 'Berlin is a city made up of bars for sad, disillusioned people to get drunk in. I've taken full advantage of working there to examine the place quite intensively. One never knows how long it's going to remain there. One fancies that it's going very fast. That's one of the reasons I was attracted to the city. It's a feeling that I really tried to capture in the paintings I did. I made a series of paintings while I was there of the Turks that live in the city. There's a track on the new album called 'Neukoln' and that's the area of Berlin where the Turks are shackled in very bad conditions.'

This new art was quite a different approach from the work he was doing in Los Angeles, where he built fifteen-foot high 'Supermen' sculptures made from polythene that he blew up with a bicycle pump. One sculpture had its foot stuck through a world globe, a babe in arms and a penis made from 3-D postcards with a Micky Mouse pencil sharpener on the end. There is no doubt that L.A. and the drugs had their effect. The new Bowie returned to German expressionism. In an interview conducted on the set of 'Just A Gigolo', David said, 'I've decided I'm a Generalist now. I think that just about covers all grounds. It encompasses anything I wish to do. I find for instance I really want to paint seriously now and not toy with it, and I am painting very seriously now, every available moment. I'd like to be known as a painter one day when I get up the nerve to show them. But I want at the moment to be known as a Generalist rather than as a singer or composer or an actor. I think a Generalist is a very good occupation to have.' At Christmas David narrated Prokofiev's 'Peter And The Wolf' for a Red Seal recording that RCA was making with Eugene Ormandy and the Philadelphia Orchestra. 'Peter And The Wolf' was his son Zowie's favourite piece of music, and so when RCA said that they were looking for someone to narrate it, David jumped at the chance.

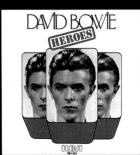

Heroes (Bowie, Eno) / **V-2 Schneider** (Bowie)
RCA PB 1121.   Released September 23, 1977.
Producers: David Bowie, Tony Visconti.
Taken from the forthcoming album 'Heroes'.
Also available on import were a variety of foreign versions of this song:
The 3.32 single in French, RCA PB 9167.
The 3.32 single in German, RCA PB 9168.
The 6.07 album track as a Spanish 12" disco cut, RCA PC 1121, which was also sent out for promotion only in the USA backed by the standard 3.32 version.
On the German pressing of the album, RCA PL 42372, Bowie sings the second half of the

Be My Wife (Bowie) / **Speed Of Life** (Bowie)
RCA PB 1017.   Released June 17, 1977.
Producers: David Bowie, Tony Visconti.
Arranger: David Bowie.
Taken from the album 'Low'.

'Low'
RCA PL 12030.   Released January 1977.
Producers: David Bowie and Tony Visconti.
Studios: The Chateau, France. Hansa By The
Wall, Berlin.
1. **Speed Of Life** (Bowie)
2. **Breaking Glass** (Bowie)
3. **What In The World** (Bowie)
4. **Sound And Vision** (Bowie)
5. **Always Crashing In The Same Car** (Bowie)
6. **Be My Wife** (Bowie)
7. **A New Career In A New Town** (Bowie)
8. **Warszawa** (Bowie, Eno)
9. **Art Decade** (Bowie)
10. **Weeping Wall** (Bowie)
11. **Subterraneans** (Bowie)
David Bowie: Vocals, ARP, tape horn and
brass, synthetic strings, saxopohones, tape
cellos, guitar, pump bass, piano, harmonica,
pre-arranged percussion, Chamberlain.
Eno: Splinter mini-Moog, Report ARP, Rimmer
EMI, EMI synthesizer, vocals, guitar
treatments, piano, Chamberlain.
Carlos Alomar: Rhythm guitars, lead guitar.

Dennis Davis: Percussion.
George Murray: Bass.
Roy Young: Piano, Farfisa organ, organ.
Ricky Gardener: Rhythm guitar, guitar.
Iggy Pop: Vocals on track 3.
Mary Visconti (Mary Hopkin): Vocals on
track 4.
Eduard Meyer: Cellos on track 9.
Peter and Paul: pianos, ARP on track 11.

'Heroes'
RCA PL 12522.   Released October 1977.
Producers: David Bowie, Tony Visconti.
Studios: Hansa By The Wall, Berlin. Mountain
Studios, Montreux, Switzerland.
1. **Beauty And The Beast** (Bowie)
2. **Joe The Lion** (Bowie)
3. **'Heroes'** (Lyrics: Bowie. Music: Bowie,
    Eno)
4. **Sons Of The Silent Age** (Bowie)
5. **Blackout** (Bowie)
6. **V-2 Schneider** (Bowie)
7. **Sense Of Doubt** (Bowie)
8. **Moss Garden** (Bowie, Eno)
9. **Neuköln** (Bowie, Eno)
10. **The Secret Life Of Arabia** (Lyrics: Bowie.
Music: Bowie, Eno, Alomar)
David Bowie: Vocals, keyboards, guitar,
saxophone, koto.
Eno: Synthesizers, keyboards, guitar
treatments.
Carlos Alomar: Rhythm guitar.
Dennis Davis: Percussion.
George Murray: Electric bass.

Robert Fripp: Lead Guitar.
Tony Visconti: Background vocals.
Antonia Maass: Background vocals.

1978 opened with David back in Berlin working on 'Just A Gigolo', preparing to co-produce Devo with Eno and getting together a world tour. He was working to such a tight schedule that he didn't even have time to meet Marlene Dietrich when they were both working on the movie.

'Just A Gigolo' was directed by David Hemmings and starred David Bowie, Marlene Dietrich, Kim Novak, Sydne Rome, Erika Pluhar and David Hemmings. It was filmed in Berlin in the winter of 1977-8 and featured David in the starring role as a young Prussian officer, Paul Von Pryzgodski, who returns penniless to Berlin after the first world war. He finds his family home rented out to whores and his mother working in a Turkish bath. After a flirtation with a street singer, played by Sydne Rome, who then goes on to become a Hollywood star he is seduced by a society matron played by fifties sexpot Kim Novak. Marlene Dietrich, making her first screen appearance since her 1961 role in 'Judgement At Nüremberg', plays the baroness who recruits him into her gigolo service.

In one scene she even sings her famous twenties song 'Pretty Gigolo, Poor Gigolo' ('Even if your heart is breaking / Show a happy face / We pay you and you must dance') from which the film was developed. All this is played out against the political unrest of the time with the left versus the burgeoning fascist party. Bowie is finally killed by a stray bullet during street fighting between the Communists and the up-and-coming Nazis. The two sides fight over his body, with the Nazis finally burying him as a martyr to a cause he never espoused.

Director David Hemmings described the film as being about a boy trying to find his own way in a time and situation which was changing so rapidly that no-one knew what he wanted. In the end all the characters opt for the easy way out.

David's much-vaunted meeting with Dietrich never happened. Dietrich refused to leave Paris where she was writing her memoirs and so the German set had to be re-constructed there. David meanwhile was by then in rehearsal for his forthcoming world tour. Their meeting on screen consists of a series of crudely edited jump shots. Dietrich is supposed to have been paid $50,000 for these scenes in a movie which itself cost $5m. 'Just A Gigolo' was premiered in Germany to resounding boos and was turned down by all the major British distributors.

It was finally taken up by Tedderwick, a new production company with Middle-Eastern backing, who immediately cut twenty minutes out of the first half of the film, making it even mcre incomprehensible than it was before. This version, shown to British critics in December 1978, was panned. Hemmings retired hurt to re-cut the movie, but it could never really be saved because the acting, with the exception of Sydne Rome, was stiff and wooden throughout from everyone.

The next project was supposed to be producing an album by Devo and even in February David was still talking about it. Michael Watts asked him why he was producing them. 'Firstly I like their music, and then meeting them had a lot to do with it. I found them very interesting people, very much in the same sort of conversational pattern as Brian and Fripp but an American equivalent. I felt there was an awful lot of enthusiasm in what they thought they could enter into eventually. The theory of their potential is very strong. I don't think it's fulfilled at this particular moment. I don't think I'm particularly interested in their basic premise of de-evolution. I just quite like their music and their lyric construction.'

But in the end the album came out crediting Brian Eno as the sole producer. David obviously had not had time to go to Cologne.

March was taken up with rehearsals for a 13-week world tour taking in 65 cities. It opened on

112

'Stage' (double)
RCA PLO2913 (2). Released October 2, 1978.
Produced by David Bowie and Tony Visconti.
Recorded live by Tony Visconti using the RCA
mobile unit during the Spring 1978 tour.
1. **Hang On To Yourself** (Bowie)
2. **Ziggy Stardust** (Bowie)
3. **Five Years** (Bowie)
4. **Soul Love** Bowie)
5. **Star** (Bowie)
6. **Station to Station** (Bowie)
7. **Fame** (Bowie, Lennon, Alomar)
8. **TVC15** Bowie
9. **Warszawa** (Bowie, Eno)
10. **Speed Of Life** (Bowie)
11. **Art Decade** (Bowie)
12. **Sense Of Doubt** (Bowie)
13. **Breaking Glass** Bowie, David, Murray)
14. **'Heroes'** (Bowie, Eno)
15. **What In The World** (Bowie)
16. **Blackout** (Bowie)
17. **Beauty And The Beast** (Bowie)
David Bowie: vocals, Chamberlain.
Carlos Alomar: rhythm guitar.

Adrian Belew: lead guitar.
Dennis David: drums, percussion.
Simon House: electric violin.
Sean Mayes: piano, string ensemble.
George Murray: bass guitar.
Roger Powell: keyboards, synthesizer.

114

March 29 in San Diego, California. The new tour was another efficient pared-down touring outfit, this time consisting of regulars George Murray on bass, Dennis Davis on drums and Carlos Alomar on rhythm guitar, to which had been added Hawkwind violinist Simon House, Roger Powell the synthesizer player, ex-Todd Rundgren's Utopia, Adrian Belew on guitar, ex of Zappa, and finally pianist Seran Mayes. David himself played a little synthesizer. It was mounted on a special little trolley for him. Under cover of darkness the band took their places on stage, and with Carlos Alomar conducting the band began by playing 'Warszawa', which was a pretty risky way to start a show. The audience understood, and were soon thrown into action by 'Heroes', which was the next in line. This was followed by 'What In The World', which gave Adrian Belew the chance to show off his guitar style. 'Be My Wife' led into 'The Jean Genie', and the huge bank of white fluorescent tubes crackled into life as the crowd cheered. Having got the crowd with him, the pace slowed for 'Blackout' and the instrumental 'Sense Of Doubt', on which David played synthesizer. He kept his trolley with him for 'Speed Of Life', then back to the mike stand for 'Breaking Glass'. 'Beauty And The Beast' was followed by 'Fame'. After an interval came a selection of Ziggy numbers, opening with 'Five Years', moving through all the familiar numbers to end with 'Ziggy Stardust' and 'Suffragette City'. The whole Ziggy sequence was a crowd stopper. David regained his breath by playing the instrumental 'Art Decade' from the 'Low' album, and then it was time for the German singalong with the Brecht/Weil 'Moon Of Alabama' (The Whisky Song). The finale was a massive version of 'Station To Station', with instrumental breaks from Powell and Belew. For encores David played 'TVC 15' and 'Stay', and as a second encore, 'Rebel Rebel'. A beautifully paced show.

The tour criss-crossed America, finally ending up with two nights at Madison Square Garden in New York City. From there they toured Europe and then, on June 14 for three nights, they played Newcastle City Hall. The music press all sent reporters there and they all filed ecstatic stories. The two-hour ten-minute concert was the best show they had seen for years, or even expected to see for years. David had reaffirmed his position in Britain, even though he hadn't toured for five years in Britain and had only done a few massive London concerts in that time.

The UK tour, its success assured, played four days at the Glasgow Apollo opening June 19th, then, after one day off, did three days at Stafford's Bingley Hall opening June 24. Then, having finally got the acoustics worked out, David concluded with three days at the giant Earls Court stadium in London. He achieved the impossible and actually managed to create an atmosphere in the huge stadium.

David's tight schedule then took him to Vienna for work on a proposed movie of the life of the Expressionist painter Egon Schiele followed by three weeks recording on his new album 'Lodger' in Switzerland where Angela and Zowie still lived in Montreux.

The year was completed by the second part of his world tour, during which he played Australia, New Zealand and Japan.

'David Bowie Narrates Prokofiev's 'Peter and the Wolf' with Eugene Ormandy and The Philadelphia Orchestra'
RCA Red Seal RL 12743.   Released May 1978.
1. **Peter And The Wolf**. Eugene Ormandy conducts the Philadelphia Orchestra, David Bowie narrator.
2. Young Person's Guide To The Orchestra by Benjamin Britten.

Beauty And The Beast (Bowie) / **Sense Of Doubt** (Bowie)
RCA PB 1190.   Released January 6, 1978.
Producers: David Bowie, Tony Visconti.
Taken from the album 'Heroes'.

1979 was a low-profile year for David. Hemmings spent January re-cutting 'Just A Gigolo' after the critics panned it, and it was premiered in February. Dull seemed to be most people's reaction. After 'Just A Gigolo' David stopped talking so much about his film career.

He was seen in public very little. In February he made a well-publicised visit to The Nashville to see the new wave electronic band The Human League, paying particular attention to the work of their video man Adrian Wright. As part of the publicity to promote 'Just A Gigolo' he did a two-hour programme on Nicky Horne's 'Your Mother Wouldn't Like It' show on Capital Radio, playing a selection of records which included Iggy, Yardbirds, The Velvet Underground, Talking Heads, La Düsseldorf, Eno and Link Wray.

March found him back in Berlin still working on the tapes for 'Lodger', the third album in the Eno trilogy. The album was originally begun in Switzerland the previous autumn, but David's tour of the Far East delayed it until then. Not all the tracks were from the Swiss and German sessions, as he mentioned in an interview, talking about the track 'Move On' from 'Lodger'. 'The interesting thing about this one is the middle section. I was playing through some old tapes of mine on a Revox and I accidentally played one backwards and I thought it was beautiful. Without listening to what it was originally we recorded the whole thing note for note backwards, and then I added vocal harmonies with Tony Visconti. If you play it backwards you'll find that it's 'All The Young Dudes'. I did this in New York, which is a very enjoyable city at the moment. It's very exciting there and is probably having its heyday as far as the arts are concerned. The whole arts thing in New York is extraordinary, much more exciting than London, which is a bit patchy. I'm so pleased that the conclusion of these three albums has been so up! You never know until you come out of the studio exactly what you've done, and I think it would be terribly depressing if the third one had been down. At least this one has a kind of optimism.'

While in New York in April, David checked out Roxy Music's New York concert and did a talk show on WPLJ-FM on which he reaffirmed that travel was his main source of material these days and not the work of other artists. 'I have to pick a city with friction in it. It has to be a city that I don't know how it works. I've got to be at odds with it. As soon as I feel comfortable I can't write in it any more. You can look back on my albums and tell which city I was in merely by just listening to them.'

'Lodger' was released on May 25th and David was in London to promote it, though he didn't show up at the launch party. The promo videos for the album were shown and were very impressive. Though Devo had already broken new ground in this field, David came up with a lot of new ideas. Instead of just playing the tracks, each one was given a new visual treatment. Thus on 'D.J.' David did a slapstick number on a radio which burst into flames. 'Look Back In Anger', one of the original titles for the album but later discarded, featured David in an artist's garret. He croons the tune while peering at a self portrait. He slowly assumes the features of the Angel of Death, picking at a few facial sores before finally collapsing. 'Boys Keep Swinging' was a typical Bowie joke. David dancing in his best funky chic Soul Train manner with a trio of female back-up singers. The trick was that the girls were all David. The first, in a black beehive hairdo and flared polka-dot dress, slinked down the catwalk then whipped off the wig and smeared the lipstick in a theatrical gesture. Then came a Lauren Bacall lookalike with blonde hair and bare shoulders in a gold lamé gown. Off came the wig and the lipstick was defiled. The final woman hobbled towards the camera on a stick wearing an old woolly cardigan. The wig stayed on and the mouth simply blew a kiss and whispered goodnight.

POST CARD.

David Bowie
c/o RCA Records,
1 Bedford Avenue,
LONDON W.C.1

LODGER

'Lodger'
RCA BOW LP 1. Released May 25, 1979
Produced by David Bowie and Tony Visconti
Engineers: Tony Visconti and David Richards.
Assistant engineer: Eugene Chaplin.
Recorded at Mountain Studios, Montreux,
Switzerland.
1. **Fantastic Voyage** (Bowie, Eno)
2. **African Night Flight** (Bowie, Eno)
3. **Move On** (Bowie)
4. **Yassassin** (Bowie)
5. **Red Sails** (Bowie, Eno)
6. **D.J.** (Bowie, Eno, Alomar)
7. **Look Back In Anger** (Bowie, Eno)
8. **Boys Keep Swinging** (Bowie, Eno)
9. **Repetition** (Bowie)
10. **Red Money** (Bowie, Alomar)
David Bowie: synthesizer on track 4, piano and
Chamberlain on tracks 1 and 6, guitar on track
10, backing vocals on tracks 1,3,4,7,8 & 10.
All lead vocals.
Dennis Davis: drums on tracks 1-7,9 and 10.
Bass on track 8.
George Murray: bass on tracks 1-7,9 and 10.

Sean Mayes: piano on tracks 1,2,3,5 and 7.
Tony Visconti: mandolin on track 1, guitar on
tracks 3 and 4, bass on track 8, backing vocals
on tracks 1,3,4,7,8 and 10.
Simon House: mandolin on track 1, violin on
tracks 4,5,8 and 9.
Adrian Belew: mandolin on track 1, guitar on
tracks 3,5,6,8,9 and 10.
Eno: ambient drone on track 1, prepared piano
and cricket menace on track 2, synthesizers
and guitar treatments on track 5, synthesizers,
horse trumpets and Eroica horn on track 7,
piano on track 8.
Carlos Alomar: guitar on tracks 2,3,4,5,6,7,9
and 10.
Stan: saxophone on track 5.
Roger Powell: synthesizer on tracks 9 and 10.

Boys Keep Swinging (Bowie)/**Fantastic Voyag**
(Bowie)
Bow 2. Released April 27, 1979.

D.J. Bowie)/**Repetition** (Bowie)
Bow 3. Released June 29, 1979.
Note: The first 75,000 copies were in a full col-
our picture sleeve.

John, I'm Only Dancing (Again) (Bowie)/**John
I'm Only Dancing** (Bowie)
7″ version: BOW 4. 12″ version: BOW 12-4.
Released December 7, 1979.
Notes: The 'A'-Side was recorded in 1975. The
'B'-Side was recorded in 1972.
The 12″ pressing was in a picture sleeve in an
edition of 50,000 plus promotional copies.

1979 closed with David singing 'Space Oddity' on Kenny Everett's New Year's Eve Show in a video clip prepared by alternating his original 1969 'Space Oddity' video with new footage of him singing in a padded cell. David told Angus MacKinnon that he only agreed to do the song, 'as long as I could do it again without all its trappings and do it strictly with three instruments. Having played it with just acoustic guitar onstage early on I was always surprised at how powerful it was just as a song without all the strings and synthesizers.' It was released as a single with a 1979 version of the Brecht-Weill 'Alabama Song' on February 15th.

There had been rumours circulating of a British tour including a week of shows at a London venue but, though he was keen to tour, he suddenly changed his mind and decided instead to revive his acting career and began reading scripts.

In February his long estranged-from relationship with Angela was finally terminated by divorce. David got custody of Zowie and Angela settled for a mere $50,000. She announced plans to write a book about her life with David saying, 'This book will make me rich' and 'Thank God this marriage is finally kaput!'

David had spent the winter travelling, first to Japan then, at Christmas, to New York to appear on the 'Saturday Night Live' TV show. While he was in New York he went to see the play 'The Elephant Man'. As he told MacKinnon; 'So I saw the thing, liked it as a piece of writing and, for myself, I thought I would have loved to have had the part if it had ever been offered to me – but it hadn't been.'

It wasn't until February, when David was back in New York doing preparatory work on the 'Scary Monsters' album that he met the director of 'The Elephant Man', Jack Hoffiss, at a party through mutual friends. 'He approached me and asked me if I would consider taking over the role at the end of the year on Broadway. I wasn't sure if I liked the idea. I wondered if he'd seen me perform or if he knew anything about me. But then he told me about my concerts and things, so he had indeed seen me – or if not, then he had a great scriptwriter. I thought that as long as he directed me I'd be quite willing to take the chance. It's the first piece of legitimate acting I've ever done, per se. So I thought I might as well. It's a very complex and difficult role, but if I was going to jump in anywhere, I might as well jump there.'

'The Elephant Man' by Bernard Pomerance is set in 19th century England and David played the lead role of Merrick, a young man, horribly deformed from birth whose body was covered with huge slabs of rotting flesh but whose mind was clear and able to reason quite normally. David played the part without the aid of horror make-up techniques. Instead he used his knowledge of mime technique to illustrate the grotesque deformities by contorting his torso and imitating Merrick's crippled walk, speaking from the side of his mouth and other mannerisms. He explained how dangerous this could be: 'I went back into mime training during rehearsal and I had to use the pre-imposed exercises before and after performances to get myself into and out of it. One's spine can be damaged very badly. I had one night of excruciating pain when I didn't do the exercises.'

Merrick was discovered in a freakshow by the eminent surgeon Frederick Treves and given rooms at The London Hospital in Whitechapel until his death in 1890 at age 27. During this period he gradually became the darling of fashionable London society. This most difficult and complex role was brilliantly acted by David, much to the surprise of the critics

1980

Space Oddity (Bowie)/**Moon Of Alabama**
(Brecht, Weill) Bow 5. Released February 15,
1980.
The version of 'Space Oddity' is the acoustic one which David performed on 'The
Kenny Everett Video Show' on New Years Eve,
1979.

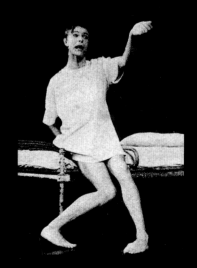

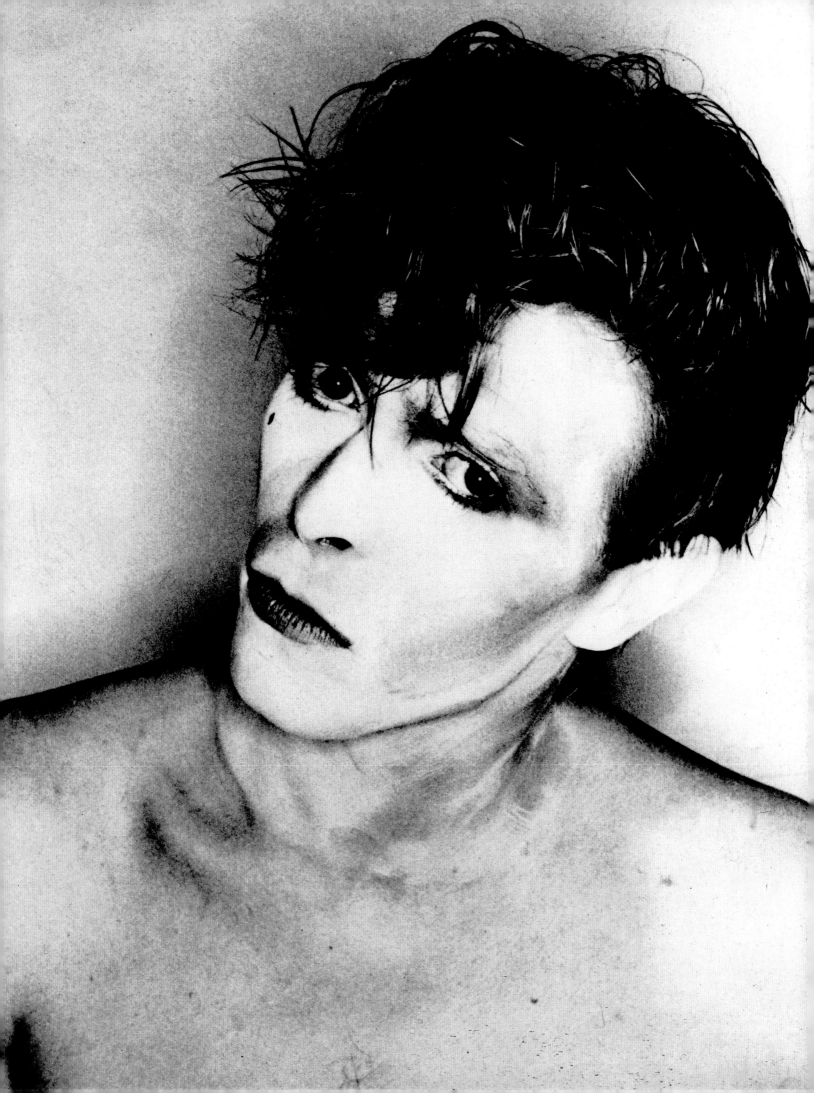

Scary Monsters
Bow LP2. Released September 12, 1980
Produced by David Bowie and Tony Visconti.
Recorded in New York City and London.
1. It's No Game (No.1) (Bowie)
2. Up The Hill Backwards (Bowie)
3. Scary Monsters (and Super Creeps) (Bowie)
4. Ashes To Ashes (Bowie)
5. Fashion (Bowie)
6. Teenage Wildlife (Bowie)
7. Scream Like A Baby (Bowie)
8. Kingdom Come (Verlaine)
9. Because You're Young (Bowie)
10. It's No Game (No.2) (Bowie)
David Bowie: vocals
Robert Fripp: guitar
Pete Townshend: guitar
Carlos Alomar: guitar
Dennis Davis: drums
George Murray: bass guitar
Roy Bittan: piano

Ashes To Ashes (Bowie)/**Move On** (Bowie)
Bow 6. Released August 1, 1980.
There were three different, though
similar, picture sleeves on this single released
in an edition of 6,000 of each in mixed lots.
Each single had with it a sheet of Bowie
stamps of which there were four possible
sheets. Therefore a record buyer would have
bought any one of a possible 12 combinations
of packaging. The 'A'-Side of the single is
taken from the forthcoming album 'Scary
Monsters'.

who were expecting another 'Just A Gigolo'. The play opened at the Center for Performing Arts in Denver, Colorado, on July 29th, and moved to Chicago's Blackstone Theater for a three week run commencing August 5th. The theatre's seating capacity was sold out and the run grossed $186,466, their biggest take ever. After a further two weeks rehearsal the play transferred to Broadway, opening September 23rd. David stayed with it and didn't give his final performance until January 4th, 1981.

In addition to walking the boards David found time to record an extraordinary new album. 'Scary Monsters (And Super Creeps)' was recorded mostly in London between May and June, produced by David and Tony Visconti. The vocal treatments represented a continuation of the work he had done with Eno but Eno was not to be found on this album – instead, such luminaries as Pete Townshend, Roy Bittan from the E Street Band and Robert Fripp fill the tracks, with Fripp playing some of the toughest guitar licks he has done in years. His best featured track, 'Fashion', was later released as a single. 'Scary Monsters (And Super Creeps)' was released on September 2nd, to a round of applause from the critics.

The first indication of the contents of 'Scary Monsters' came with the release on August 1st of 'Ashes To Ashes' in which David resurrects one of his first characters, Major Tom, the hero of his first hit, 'Space Oddity'. Things have changed though and the heroic Major Tom is now a junkie...'Originally Major Tom was a magnificent and heroic figure who would win all battles,' recalled David, 'but as the song progressed he turned into pretty much of a wimp. The luck generally seemed to be sad. 'Ashes To Ashes' is about the dissolution of the great dream that brought Major Tom to space in the first place. Ten years later everything has soured, because there was no reason to put him up there in the first place – just an ego trip.

'Everybody uses noble phrases like 'the betterment of mankind' when they talk about space exploration, and I am sure that there are some good souls involved with the project. But I don't anticipate that it will open up new worlds or change the mess we have gotten ourselves into. On the whole it just seems like some place higher to jump from.'

The video that accompanied the release of 'Ashes to Ashes' was quite revolutionary. It never quite followed the story line of the song but provided a visual counterpoint. 'To just illustrate the song in terms of itself would be a disastrous idea,' David explained, 'because people have well-formulated inner ideas of what a song should look like. I try to work against the music, to work out a story line which is not going to just illustrate the song word-for-word, but develop a counter-idea that has the same kind of weight but deals with different character situations.'

In July David returned to Japan. He didn't just visit his girlfriend, while there he made a television commercial for the Japanese alcoholic drink, sake. 'There are three reasons why I've done this. The first being that no-one has ever asked me to do it before. And the money is very useful. And the third, I think it's very effective that my music is on the television twenty times a day. I think my music isn't for radio.'

The commercial was shot in a temple in Kyoto and took two weeks to complete starting each day at 5am. David appeared at a piano wearing a white satin shirt. He held up a glass of sake and said, 'Crystal Jun Rock In Japan' while his 'Crystal Japan' instrumental played behind him. This instrumental was sold in the UK on an RCA import and was released in Britain in 1981 as the B-side of 'Up The Hill Backwards'.

Fashion (Bowie)/**Scream Like A Baby**
(Bowie)
BOW T7. Released October 1980.

RCA
SS-3270
(JPBO-8156)

美しい主旋律の中に光る純粋で透明な世界！　　宝焼酎"純"イメージ曲　　¥600

クリスタル・ジャパン

デビッド・ボウイー

DAVID BOWIE
CRYSTAL JAPAN

ALABAMA SONG
アラバマ・ソング

THE BEST OF
Bowie

'The Best of David Bowie'
K-Tel NE 1111. Released December 1980.
1. Space Oddity
2. Life On Mars
3. Starman
4. Rock 'n' Roll Suicide
5. John I'm Only Dancing
6. Jean Genie
7. Breaking Glass
8. Sorrow
9. Diamond Dogs
10. Young Americans
11. Fame
12. Golden Years
13. TVC 15
14. Sound And Vision
15. Heroes
16. Boys Keep Swinging

Nothing was seen of David in public until February 24th when he appeared at the New London Theatre to collect his award of 'Best Male Singer of 1980' from disc jockey Dave Lee Travis and Lulu. David didn't reveal much, 'I'd like to take this opportunity of not saying very much...But, thank you very much. I do appreciate it.' He gave a big grin and left leaving Travis somewhat nonplussed.

David was next sighted in July, at The Embassy Club in Bond Street. He and Pete Townshend had been together in the studio where Pete was recording a solo album. David was sporting a half grown beard in preparation for his role in the BBC TV play of Bertold Brecht's 'Baal'. This minor work, Brecht's first play, marked David's television acting début. He played the leading role, that of Herbert Beerbolm Baal, an anarchist poet who attacks bourgeois gentility by being an abusive, alcoholic vagabond. David described Baal to The Soho News in New York: 'Baal is the kind of person I've been avoiding in bars for years. Sometimes we get talking though, and the interesting bits sort of stick. I thought I could identify with the character once removed.'

129

In September David returned to New York where he attended The Rolling Stones' Madison Square Garden concert, going backstage afterwards and having a night out on the town with Mick Jagger. In an interview, Jagger revealed that he and David were considering ideas for a film together: 'David has some funny ideas and we've been trying to write an original screenplay together. It has a real chance of happening. It will be a small budget fun thing rather than a big Hollywood production. I also have an idea for a small musical without the band. A bit like the kind of thing Bowie used to do or similar to Bette Midler's show only not so camp.'

David returned to Montreux and his son. In October Roger Deacon, drummer with Queen, was in Montreux with the group to work out some ideas for a new studio album. He had been a friend of David's for some time and a telephone call resulted in a meeting in which David and all four members of Queen wrote a song together and recorded it on the spot. Freddie Mercury was reported as saying that it was 'one of the best things that Queen has ever done'. The single, 'Under Pressure' was released in November with a Queen number on the flip-side.

On December 17th, 'Christiane F.', the movie, was released in Britain featuring David in a special concert sequence. The film, about a teenage drug addict in Berlin, became the most commercially successful German film ever.

For Bowie watchers 1981 was a particularly uneventful year with no concerts and not even a new album for them to examine.

1981

130

AS BAAL. (PHOTO: BBC).

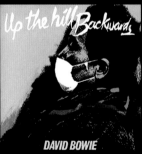

Scary Monsters (And Super Creeps)
(Bowie)/**Because You're Young** (Bowie)
BOW 8.   Released January 1981.

Up The Hill Backwards/Crystal Japan
RCA BOW 9.   Released March 1981.

Under Pressure (Bowie)/**Soul Brother**
(Queen)
EMI 5250.   Released November 1981.
A-side features Bowie duetting with
Freddie Mercury of Queen; B-side features
Queen alone.

'Christiane F. Wir Kinder Vom Bahnhof Zoo'
RCA BL 43606 (Germany).   Released May 1981.
1. **V-2 Schneider**
2. **TVC 15**
3. **Heroes**
4. **Boys Keep Swinging**
5. **Sense of Doubt**
6. **Station To Station**
7. **Look Back In Anger**
8. **Stay**
9. **Warszawa**
Bowie's music was chosen as the soundtrack for this German film. RCA Germany released the album and RCA UK imported 25,000 copies.

The first Bowie record of the year was released on February 20th. It was an EP containing the five Brecht songs sung by David in the TV play Baal which was transmitted on March 2nd. The play, Brecht's first and certainly not his finest, was a curious vehicle for David to choose for his TV acting début. The production used the latest video techniques, including split screen, but ultimately it was not a memorable experience and even David's acting was indifferent.

On March 1st David began work on 'The Hunger', a horror film directed by Tony Scott from the novel by Whitley Streiber, co-starring Catherine Deneuve. Location filming took place in a mansion in Curzon Street, Mayfair, in the original setting of Bram Stoker's 'Dracula' in Whitby and in the gay nightclub, Heaven, where David and Catherine Deneuve as present day vampires stalked their prey while Pete Murphy of Bauhaus performed. For an eighteenth century sequence, David and Catherine were filmed at Luton Hoo in period costumes—the house was closed but the gardens remained open to the public who were unaware of what what was happening inside.

In July, the famous ageing sequence was filmed, in which David appeared to age three hundred years in a matter of minutes. It was shot in a closed set, made extra secure by David's two personal bodyguards who were present throughout production.

During his stay in London David rented a flat in Belgravia and in July there was a press report that he and tennis star John McEnroe had taken tea together. McEnroe was renting the flat next door and had disturbed David's sleep with tortuous renderings of David's 'Rebel Rebel' and the Stones' 'Satisfaction'. David introduced himself and showed McEnroe the correct chords.

He was also seen out on the town at Gossips, where he got drunk with three members of Exploited and Gene October from Chelsea. He attended the première of the Ballet Rambert's 'Berlin Requiem' at Sadler's Wells, showed up at a Design For Living gig at The Roebuck pub on Tottenham Court Road and, in the company of Catherine Deneuve, saw Glenda Jackson and Georgina Hale in the comedy 'Summit Conference' at the Lyric Theatre, Shaftesbury Avenue.

No sooner had David completed work on 'The Hunger' than it was announced that he was to play a major role in Nagisa Oshima's new film 'Merry Christmas Mr. Lawrence', playing alongside Tom Conti and Riuichi Sakamoto from The Yellow Magic Orchestra. The film is

1982

134

WITH CATHERINE DEVENUE.

Baal EP
RCA BOW 11.   Released February 1982.
Producers: Bowie & Tony Visconti.
1   **Baal's Hymn** (Bertolt Brecht/Dominic
     Muldowney)
2   **Remembering Marie A** (Brecht/
     Muldowney)
3   **Ballad Of The Adventurers** (Brecht/
     Muldowney)
4   **The Drowned Girl** (Brecht/Kurt Weill)
5   **The Dirty Song** (Brecht/Muldowney)
Songs from the TV film of Brecht's first
play in which Bowie acted the title role.

**Peace On Earth/Little Drummer Boy/
Fantastic Voyage**
BOW 12.   Released November 1982.
First two tracks feature Bowie duetting
with Bing Crosby

taken from Laurens Van Der Post's short story 'A Bar Of Shadow' contained in 'The Seed And The Sower' collection, and deals with the relationship between a British prisoner of war and a Japanese guard. The reasons behind the Japanese cruelty to enemies that allow themselves to be captured alive are explained in an analysis of Japanese traditions and culture. This attempt to understand the apparent sadism of the Japanese caused controversy when the book was first published shortly after the war.

Oshima is one of the best known and respected of Japan's directors, known to most Europeans for 'In The Realm Of The Senses' and 'The Ceremony'. 'Merry Christmas Mr. Lawrence' was the first ever Anglo-Japanese film production. Bowie plays the role of the POW, a difficult and demanding job which he achieved masterfully. The film was shot in New Zealand, the Cook Islands and in Tokyo. David's work on the film took from early September until early November when David went to New York to complete the preparations for a new studio album. Meanwhile, RCA released the 'Fashions' picture disc pack containing ten of David's old singles in a very attractive picture disc form and followed this on November 18th by releasing a Christmas single of David singing with Bing Crosby. This unlikely record contained versions of 'Peace On Earth', 'Little Drummer Boy' and 'Fantastic Voyage' and was taken from Crosby's December 1977 Christmas television show in the States. It reached number three in the UK charts.

Space Oddity/Changes/Velvet Goldmine
RCA BOWP 101
Life On Mars/The Man Who Sold The World
RCA BOWP 102
Jean Genie/Ziggy Stardust
RCA BOWP 103
Rebel Rebel/Queen Bitch
RCA BOWP 104
Sound And Vision/A New Career In A New Town
RCA BOWP 105
Drive In Saturday/Round And Round
RCA BOWP 106
Sorrow/Amsterdam
RCA BOWP 107
Golden Years/Can You Hear Me
RCA BOWP 108
Boys Keep Swinging/Fantastic Voyage
RCA BOWP 109
Ashes To Ashes/Move On
RCA BOWP 110
All released November 1982.
Limited edition set of picture singles

Early in the New Year David booked into a New York studio to begin recording 'Let's Dance', his first album of original material since 'Scary Monsters' in 1980. Tony Visconti, his long serving record producer, was replaced by disco auteur Nile Rodgers and apart from guitarist Carlos Alomar the musicians he choose to work with were all fresh names: bassist Carmine Rojas, drummers Omar Hakim and Tony Thompson, guitarist Stevie Ray Vaughn and keyboard player Rob Sabind.

David's contract with RCA had now expired and negotiations were under way with Bhasker Menon, the chairman of EMI America. On January 21st the deal was signed: a five year commitment to furnish EMI America (and the UK EMI company) with five albums for what was rumoured to be a $10,000,000 advance against future royalties. EMI were overjoyed and Bhasker Menon arranged a press conference with David to announce it.

The break from RCA was predictable. David was known to have been dissatisfied with his old record outlet for some time. He talked about it in an interview with David Thomas: 'It was just a question of non co-operation with each other by the end of that contract. It was a ten year experience–just a weeny bit too long. And the turnover of personnel at RCA was just so absurd that there was no continuity.' At his London press conference later in the year David said: 'I didn't like RCA because they didn't like me. I think I released several very interesting, intelligent and important albums at RCA which they didn't have much time for. We both felt it was time we forgot about each other.'

Such sentiments did not discourage RCA from releasing a 'new' David Bowie album that same month. 'Bowie Rare' was a compilation of 11 tracks which were not so much rare as currently difficult to obtain in original or subsequent pressings. Assembled by RCA's Italian office, the record included a number of novelty items like 'Ragazzo Solo, Ragazza Sola' ('Space Oddity' set to an Italian lyric), 'Helden' (the German version of 'Heroes'), the sake commercial 'Crystal Japan' and a number of B-sides and alternative takes of already familiar material.

In March, immediately after completing 'Let's Dance', David flew to Australia to work on promotional videos for the title track–soon to be released as a single–and 'China Girl', a song written with Iggy Pop in 1977 and recorded by Iggy on his album 'The Idiot'. He was accompanied by his son Zowie, who now answered to the name of Joey, and London based film director David Mallet who worked up a story line for the two short films.

The 'Let's Dance' video featured two students from Sydney's Aboriginal-Islanders Dance Theatre, a boy named Terry Roberts and a girl named Jolene King, while the 'China Girl' sequence co-starred a stunningly attractive Oriental girl from New Zealand named Geeling. Both videos carried a strong anti-racist message: 'They're almost like Russian social realism, very naïve...and the message they have is very simple–it's wrong to be racist,' David told Rolling Stone writer Kurt Loder during the filming. 'I thought, let's try to use the video format as a platform for some kind of social observation and not just waste it on trying to enhance the public image of the singer involved.'

Nevertheless the 'China Girl' video, which featured an apparently naked Bowie canoodling in the surf with Geeling, upset the BBC back in England. The offending scenes were edited out for showing on Top Of The Pops though the uncensored version was screened on other, less discreet, TV programmes.

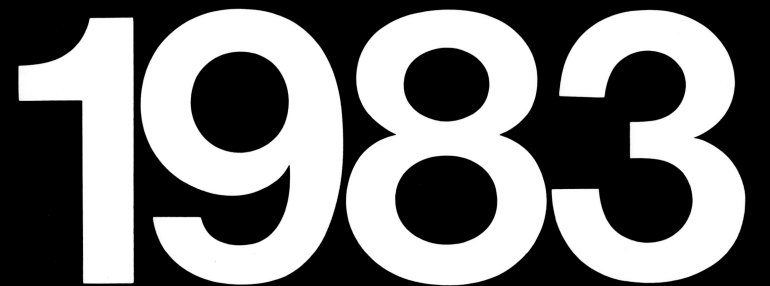

1983

BOWIE

'Bowie Rare'
RCA PL 45406. Released January 1983.
1.   **Ragazzo Solo, Ragazza Sola** (Bowie)
2.   **Round And Round** (Chuck Berry)
3.   **Amsterdam** (Jacques Brel)
4.   **Holy Holy** (Bowie)
5.   **Panic In Detroit** (Bowie)
6.   **Young Americans** (Bowie)
7.   **Velvet Goldmine** (Bowie)
8.   **Helden** (Bowie)
9.   **John I'm Only Dancing (Again)** (1975)
     (Bowie)
10. **Moon Of Alabama** (Brecht-Weill)
11. **Crystal Japan** (Bowie)

The single version of 'Let's Dance', coupled with the equally impressive 'Cat People', was released on March 14th. It was an immediate and predictable success, topping the UK charts within two weeks of release and staying there for most of April. On March 26th David flew into London for a press conference at the swish Claridges Hotel, an event covered in great detail by the music press and featured on BBC 2's Newsnight programme later the same evening. Despite his 26-hour plane flight David looked as fresh as a daisy with stylishly cut blonde hair swept into a casual quiff, his skin lightly tanned from the Australian experience, his fashionable fawn suit and loosely knotted tie offering just the right touch of informal elegance that the occasion demanded.

The main business of the press conference was to announce concert plans – his first in five years – but those who anticipated a full scale UK tour were to be disappointed. Instead David planned a swing through Europe that included three shows at London's Wembley Empire Pool (June 2nd, 3rd, & 4th) and two at Birmingham's National Exhibition Centre (June 5th & 6th). The opening concert was set for Frankfurt on May 20th and other Continental venues on the itinerary included Munich, West Berlin, Bad Segerberg, Offenbach, Bochum, Rotterdam, Brussels, Lyon, Fréjus and Paris. Playing alongside David would be a ten-piece band comprising Stevie Ray Vaughn and Carlos Alomar (guitars), Carmine Rojas (bass), Tony Thompson (drums), Fred Mandell (keyboards) plus a horn section and back-up vocalists. In the event Vaughn was replaced by long serving Bowie sideman Earl Slick at the last minute.

'This is the first concert tour I've done in five or six years so for me it's more than exciting, it's kind of terrifying at the same time and that, possibly, can help the performance', David told the assembled gathering.

Three weeks later, after much speculation in the press, it was announced that David would play three open-air concerts at Milton Keynes Concert Bowl on July 1st, 2nd and 3rd. For the rest of July and August he would tour North America and, later in the year, perform in Australia and Japan. The total number of concerts scheduled was ninety.

In early May, just before the start of the concert tour, David was in Cannes to promote his two upcoming films – 'The Hunger' and 'Merry Christmas Mr. Lawrence' – at the annual Film Festival. Though the immediate future would be dominated by his lucrative musical endeavours, it was clear that in the long term David regarded his acting work as equally, if not more, important.

Throughout spring David was rarely off the front pages; his profile had never been higher. The 'Let's Dance' album was released to glowing reviews on April 14th and, like the single, it rapidly ascended the charts on both sides of the Atlantic. It was his most accessible album in years, a snappy blend of soul, hard rock and techno-pop. 'I'm just a little tired of experimentation now,' he told NME's Chris Bohn in April. 'But electronics are rewarding in terms of playing around with atmosphere and trying to reach different parts of the mind, funny corners of the mind...that's why I've used a very organic, basic instrumentation on this new album.

'I think the music I'm writing at the moment is probably going to reach a newer audience for me. But if I am going to reach a new audience then I'm going to try and reach it with something to say...I don't want to be the grandfather of the new wave by any means.'

'Let's Dance'
EMI AML 3029.   Released April 1983.
Producers: Bowie & Nile Rodgers.
1. **Modern Love** (Bowie)
2. **China Girl** (Bowie/Iggy Pop)
3. **Let's Dance** (Bowie)
4. **Without You** (Bowie)
5. **Ricochet** (Bowie)
6. **Criminal World** (Peter Godwin/Duncan Browne/Sean Lyons)
7. **Cat People** (Putting Out Fire) (Bowie/ Moroder)
8. **Shake It** (Bowie)
Carmine Rojas: Bass.
Omar Hakim: Drums.
Nile Rodgers: Guitar.
Stevie Ray Vaughn: Lead guitar.
Rob Sabind: Keyboards.
Mac Gollehon: Trumpet.
Robert Arron: Tenor, Flute.
Stan Harrison: Tenor, Flute.
Steve Elson: Baritone, Flute.
Sammy Figueroa: Percussion.

Let's Dance (Bowie)/**Cat People (Putting Out Fire)** (Bowie/Georgio Moroder)
EMI EA 152.   Released April 1983.
Produced by David Bowie and Nile Rodgers.

China Girl (Bowie/Pop)/**Shake It** (Bowie)
EMI EA 157.   Released May 1983.

Modern Love (Bowie)/**Modern Love** (live version)
EMI EA 158.   Released September 1983.

142

'Ziggy Stardust –The Motion Picture'
RCA PL 84862 (2).   Released November 1983.
Producers: David Bowie & Mike Moran.
1. **Hang On To Yourself** (Bowie)
2. **Ziggy Stardust** (Bowie)
3. **Watch That Man** (Bowie)
4. **Medley: Wild Eyed Boy From Freecloud** (Bowie)/**All The Young Dudes** (Bowie)/**Oh You Pretty Thing** (Bowie)
5. **Moonage Daydream** (Bowie)
6. **Space Oddity** (Bowie)
7. **My Death** (Jacques Brel/Mort Shuman/ Eric Blau)
8. **Cracked Actor** (Bowie)
9. **Time** (Bowie)
10. **Width Of A Circle** (Bowie)
11. **Changes** (Bowie)
12. **Let's Spend The Night Together** (Jagger/Richards)
13. **Suffragette City** (Bowie)
14. **White Light/White Heat** (Lou Reed)
15. **Rock 'n' Roll Suicide** (Bowie)

Mick Ronson: Guitar, Vocals.
Trevor Bolder: Bass.
Woody Woodmansey: Drums.
Ken Fordham: Saxophone.
Brian Wilshaw: Horns.
John Hutchinson: Guitar.
Geoff MacCormack: Back-up vocals, Percussion.
Mike Garson: Piano.

The interview ranged over many subjects – his recent acting roles, racism in Australia, the joys and responsibilities of parenthood and, largely as an aside, his recent music. He was unusually warm about Joey.

'I would never have thought it possible but for me the one most enjoyable and hope giving quality of life over the past four or five years is my son,' he told Bohn. 'When the son gets to the age of nine, 10, 11 and 12 and starts asking those really inquisitive, curious and unanswerable questions, well, my response has been to consider how important life is, and how important it is for him. And as it became more important for him through me, I found it became more important for me as well. And our future collectively started taking precedence over everything else. That's had a very strong bearing on what I intend to do in the future. I feel I have to make a commitment to something more altruistic to that which I've been concerned with before.'

Bohn offered Bowie an opportunity to recant on his fascist leanings of 1976 – he required little encouragement – and the topic swung into a condemnation not only of ultra-Right politics but also of drugs. 'Drugs are no part of my writing or recording or anything,' he said. 'It's impossible to consider your life worthwhile, or the life of those around you worthwhile, if you're just fractured like that. I mean . . . God knows what would have happened to my son if I was continually stoned for the last 10 years. I probably wouldn't have him. He certainly wouldn't have wanted me . . . I'm quite sure about that.'

In May, just before the start of the Serious Moonlight Tour, Bowie was in Cannes to lend his support to the launch of both 'The Hunger' and 'Merry Christmas Mr Lawrence' at the Film Festival. He shared a rostrum with Oshima to discuss the latter, and seemed as adept at dealing with film writers as he had become at dealing with music writers over the years. But the Cannes Film Festival was Bowie's last glance at the film industry for some time to come: for the next eight months Bowie was the eye in the hurricane which swept through 15 countries and touched the lives of over two and a half million fans.

The Serious Moonlight Tour opened in Brussels on May 18 and closed in Hong Kong on December 8. In the meantime it visited 59 cities in three continents where 96 concerts were performed. The European leg included three shows at London's Wembley Empire Pool, two at

White Light/White Heat (Lou Reed)/
Cracked Actor (Bowie)
RCA 372.   Released November 1983.

White Light/White Heat

Birmingham's National Exhibition Centre and – after much speculation and delay in their announcement – three open air shows at the Milton Keynes Concert Bowl. Accompanying Bowie was a 10-piece band: Earl Slick and Carlos Alomar on guitars, Carmine Rojas on bass, Tony Thompson on drums, Fred Mandell on keyboards plus a horn section and back-up vocalists. Slick was a late replacement for Stevie Ray Vaughan who pulled out at the last minute after a bitter and widely reported dispute over his salary which was never resolved.

Vaughan's abrupt departure was the only unforeseen problem during manoeuvres that were co-ordinated with ruthless efficiency by a small army of permanent or transient employees dedicated to the Bowie cause in 1983. 'Let's Dance', the album, was released in April, a month before touring began, and its success in the marketplace was partly a reflection of Bowie's high profile and partly a reflection of the accessible music therein.

The r&b and raunchy rock 'n' roll which Bowie favoured on his South Seas trip was evident from the opening track 'Modern Love' to the closing 'Shake It'. Eminently commercial, most of the music from 'Let's Dance' was ideal for live performance and four tracks – 'Modern Love', 'China Girl', 'Cat People' and the title song – were included in the Serious Moonlight programme. EMI must have been delighted with their acquisition, especially since Bowie's sales graph at RCA had see-sawed alarmingly in recent years.

Reviews of the album were largely favourable and the concerts were greeted with similar enthusiasm. Much thought had gone into the presentation, and Bowie's cosmopolitan leanings were reflected in both the music and the dress of the musicians: Rojas and Alomar in African look, Slick in rock-style headband, jeans and open shirt, and Bowie himself the elegant Englishman in lightweight suit and loosely knotted bow tie. Eric Barrett, Bowie's long established lighting engineer, produced a stunning display courtesy of a backstage computer, and the programme reached back to include music from all stages of Bowie's career.

The sets varied little from night to night or country to country. Aside from the four new songs, concert goers were treated to 'Jean Genie', 'Star', 'Heroes', 'Wild Is The Wind', 'Golden Years', 'Fashion', 'Breaking Glass', 'Life On Mars', 'Sorrow', 'Scary Monsters', 'Rebel Rebel', 'White Light White Heat', 'Station To Station', 'Cracked Actor', 'Ashes To Ashes', 'Space Oddity', 'Young Americans', 'Fame', 'TVC 15' and 'Hang On To Yourself'.

'White Light White Heat' closed the first half of each show and was given over to the band for whatever improvisation occurred on a given night. Many shows closed with a full tilt version of The Who's 'I Can't Explain' which, like 'Sorrow', Bowie had covered on 'Pin Ups'.

The English and European dates were heavily over-subscribed which gave touts a field day for the London concerts at Wembley where reviewers complained of a muddy sound. There were complaints, too, about the high ticket price and the exorbitant prices charged at the merchandising stand for t-shirts and programmes. A special charity performance was arranged for Hammersmith Odeon on June 30 when the cream of rock nobility paid £50 a ticket which went to the Brixton Neighbourhood Community Association – Bowie's birthplace.

In July Bowie's face adorned the front page of Time magazine and the American concerts were greeted with even more critical acclaim than those in the UK. Stars from stage, screen and sports field applied anxiously for tickets for both Madison Square Garden and the Los Angeles Forum and among those who attended were Mick Jagger, Michael Jackson, Keith Richards, John McEnroe, Raquel Welch, Sting, Cher, Bette Midler, Duran Duran, Shelley Duval, David Hemmings, Jaclyn Smith, Henry Winkler, Richard Gere and Susan Sarandon. Bowie's old sparring partner Mick

Ronson showed up in Toronto and was coaxed on to the stage to jam during 'Jean Genie'.

The touring party took a month's break during September before reconvening on October 16 in Tokyo for the start of the Far East leg. Australia and New Zealand followed before Serious Moonlight finally drew to a close with shows in Bangkok and Hong Kong. With the possible exception of the Rolling Stones' global extravaganza of 1981/2, it was the largest tour ever undertaken by any rock performer.

The Japanese leg of the tour was particularly eventful, and the warmth with which Bowie was received had much to do with his fluent Japanese language introductions during several concerts. At a Tokyo press conference on October 18 he was reunited with various members of the cast of 'Merry Christmas Mr Lawrence', and an hour-long TV special was later broadcast in his honour. Inevitably 'China Girl' proved a crowd favourite, especially as Bowie often changed the lyrics to 'My little Japanese girl' or 'My little Nippon girl'.

On October 30, following a huge outdoor performance, an earthquake shook the Tokyo hotel where Bowie was staying. He was, by all accounts, the calmest member of the party, and as hotel guests congregated in the lobby to sit out the danger Bowie quipped that the earthquake was a publicity stunt by EMI for 'Shake It'.

It was characteristic that such a hectic six months of activity should be followed by a lengthy silence and throughout the first half of 1984 Bowie maintained the low profile at which he has become increasingly adept. He showed little interest in 'Ziggy Stardust – The Motion Picture' and its accompanying live album on RCA, both of which emerged at the end of 1983.

This was director D.A. Pennebaker's documentary film account of the events surrounding Bowie's 1973 concert at London's Hammersmith Odeon: the night of July 3 when he said farewell to Ziggy Stardust and The Spiders From Mars. The footage and tapes had been kicking around for ages, and for more recent Bowie fans who had thrilled to Serious Moonlight the 1973 image was disorientating to say the least. RCA also chose to release a single of Bowie's version of 'White Light White Heat', the Lou Reed song he resurrected during 1983.

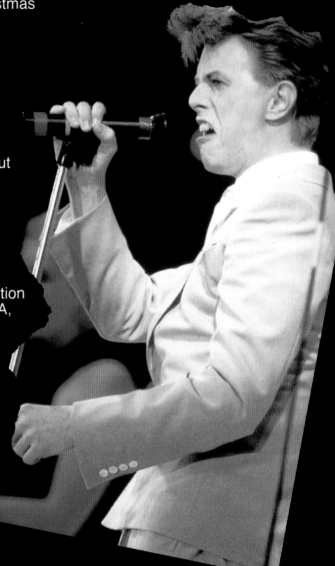

48

'Love You Till Tuesday'
Decca Bowie 1. Released May 1984.
Producers: Mike Vernon, Ken Pitt, Leslie
Conn.
1. **Love You Till Tuesday** (Bowie)
2. **Sell Me A Coat** (Bowie)
3. **When I'm Five** (Bowie)
4. **Rubber Band** (Bowie)
5. **Let Me Sleep Beside You** (Bowie)
6. **Ching-A-Ling Song** (Bowie)
7. **Space Oddity** (original version)
    (Bowie)
8. **When I Live My Dream** (remix)
    (Bowie)
9. **The Laughing Gnome** (Bowie)
10. **Liza Jane** (Leslie Conn)
    A re-issue of Bowie's (selected)
    material on Decca to accompany the
    release of the film of the same name.

Blue Jean (Bowie)/**Dancing With The
Big Boys** (Bowie)
EMI America EA 181. Released
September 1984.

Blue Jean/Dancing With The Big Boys
(remix)/**Dancing With The Big Boys**
(extended)
EMI America 12EA 181 12″. Released
September 1984.

Tonight (Bowie/Iggy Pop)/**Tumble And
Twirl** (Bowie/Iggy Pop)
EMI America EA 187. Released
November 1984.

Tonight/Tumble And Twirl
EMI America 12EA 187 12″. Released
November 1984.

Early in the New Year it was reported that Bowie would play the Pied Piper of Hamelin for 'Faery Tale Theatre', an American cable TV series, but these plans were cancelled in favour of recording sessions at the Mountain studios near Montreux. There was also talk of Bowie appearing in the new film of '1984' alongside John Hurt and Richard Burton, and as a villain in the next James Bond movie. Again, both turned out to be only rumours. Meanwhile there appeared on the market the first of two videos from the Serious Moonlight Tour as well as 'Ziggy Stardust – The Motion Picture' on video, and the soundtrack to the ancient but only recently released 'Love You On Tuesday' which included his first ever single 'Liza Jane'. The second part of the Serious Moonlight video was released later in the year.

The Montreux recording sessions were relocated to Marin Heights near Toronto in the spring and a new producer, Derek Bramble, supervised the recording of what would become September's 'Tonight' album. In the past Bramble had played for the UK soul band Heatwave and worked with ex-Linx frontman David Grant. Another close ally was Bowie's old friend Iggy Pop.

'I really wanted to work with Iggy again . . . that's something I've not done for a long time,' Bowie told NME's Charles Shaar Murray the following September. 'We're ultimately leading up, I hope, to me doing Iggy's next album. We've been talking about it for a year or so.'

The Iggy collaborations were symptomatic of the album as a whole in that there was a marked absence of Bowie's own writing (there were two older covers as well). 'I wanted to keep my hand in, so to speak, and go back in the studio but I didn't really feel like I had enough new things of my own because of the tour,' he told Murray.

'I can't write on tour and there wasn't really enough preparation afterwards to write anything that I felt was really worth putting down, and I didn't want to put out things that 'would do'. There were two or three that I felt were good things to do, and the other stuff.'

The single released from the album, 'Blue Jean', was a Bowie composition and far and away the most likely commercial hit on the LP. For an accompanying video, all 22 minutes of it, Bowie commissioned director Julien Temple, the 30-year-old whizz-kid responsible for The Sex Pistols' 'Great Rock 'n' Roll Swindle' and who was currently working on a film version of Colin MacInnes' novel 'Absolute Beginners'. In 'Jazzin' For Blue Jean' Bowie took two roles, that of a painted and dissipated rock star (Screaming Lord Byron) and a hapless would-be Romeo called Vic who assumes that by taking his dreamboat to see and meet Byron she will melt in his arms. The opposite happens, of course, with Byron stealing the girl from beneath Vic's slightly misshapen nose. 'Jazzin' For Blue Jean' was premièred in the UK on September 21 as support to the film 'The Company Of Wolves'.

The album was greeted with mixed reviews and a general consensus opining that Bowie was treading water between the monumental success of 'Let's Dance' and his third EMI LP which would herald another tour.

By Bowie's standards 'Tonight' was only a modest commercial success but such matters were of little import. 'The interesting thing about rock,' he told Shaar Murray over tea in The Savoy Hotel, 'is that you never think it's going on for much longer. Then you find out that it has . . . I'm 37 going on 38 and I find myself thinking . . . "I'm still doing it."

'So you're re-defining it all the time. The whole animal of rock keeps changing itself so fast and so furiously that you just can't plan ahead. I've got absolutely no idea. I've got two or three anchors: to do some more work with Iggy and to try and write something for myself that is extraordinary and adventurous. Those are the only things in music that I know I'll be doing in future.'

THE JAZZING FOR BLUE JEAN VIDEO. (PHOTO: REX FEATURES)

'Tonight'
EMI America DB 1. Released September 1984.
Producers: David Bowie, Derek Bramble, Hugh Padgham.
1. **Loving The Alien** (Bowie)
2. **Don't Look Down** (Iggy Pop/James Williamson)
3. **God Only Knows** (Brian Wilson/ Tony Asher)
4. **Tonight** (Bowie/Iggy Pop)
5. **Neighbourhood Threat** (Bowie/Iggy Pop)
6. **Blue Jean** (Bowie)
7. **Tumble And Twirl** (Bowie/Iggy Pop)
8. **I Keep Forgettin'** (Jerry Leiber/Mike Stoller)
9. **Dancing With The Big Boys** (Bowie/Iggy Pop/Carlos Alomar)
Carlos Alomar: Guitars.
Derek Bramble: Bass guitar, Guitar, Synthesizer.

Carmine Rojas: Bass guitar.
Sammy Figueroa: Percussion.
Omar Hakim: Drums.
Guy St Onge: Marimba.
Robin Clark, George Simms, Curtis King: Vocals.

There was, after the success of Serious Moonlight, little need for David to exert himself. He'd become considerably richer than at any time in his life and the intervening years seemed only to have added to his uncommon physical beauty. He was now amongst the world's most eligible bachelors whose constant companions were his teenage son, to whom he was a devoted and conscientious father, and his personal assistant Corinne ('Coco') Schwab, a girl of multifarious talents whose slavish devotion to her master had become quite legendary. He was a man of truly international citizenship with homes in Scotland, Switzerland (where he spent most of his time) and New York City. Bowie guarded his privacy jealously, with the result that public appearances, for whatever reason and however inconsequential, became events worthy of considerable newspaper coverage. Actual interviews were now becoming rarer and rarer, virtually annual events, timed always to coincide with – and consequently assist – commercial endeavours.

The only fly in the ointment, as 1985 wore on, was a series of articles in The Sunday Times, excerpts from a forthcoming book, which probed deeply into Bowie's personal life and relationship with his family, notably his step-brother Terry Jones who died earlier in the year by his own hand. Terry had a history of mental illness and the authors of these articles, ST writer Peter Gillman and his wife Leni, uncovered a long history of such illness in his mother's family. Their conclusion, almost inevitably, was that David was concerned that he might become a victim of this family 'curse' himself.

The word from the Bowie camp was that David abhorred the articles. There was even talk that he would sue The Sunday Times.

Such matters were far from David's mind on July 13, the day of the Live Aid concert at Wembley Stadium, perhaps the greatest ever line-up of pop and rock talent. Gathering around him a band of young and eager players, including keyboard and synthesizer specialist Thomas Dolby, Bowie's set was unquestionably a highlight in a day to remember.

He performed just four songs – 'TVC 15', 'Jean Genie', 'Modern Love' and 'Heroes' – but their presentation demonstrated that Bowie was a consummate professional who took the event very seriously indeed. Much rehearsal had gone into this 15-minute plus performance and, instead of

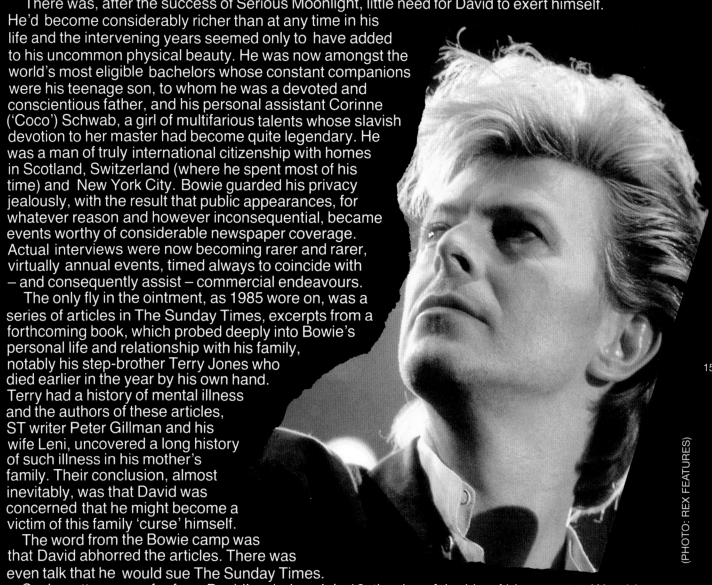

(PHOTO: REX FEATURES)

1985

performing a fifth song, David introduced a harrowing film of starving Ethiopian children which was simulcast on video screens for the live audience. He dedicated the marvellous reading of 'Heroes' to . . . 'my son, your children and the children of the world,' and after his set told backstage interviewer Paul Gambaccini that he thought Live Aid should be an annual event. It was clear that he was much moved by the occasion and that his input had helped organiser Bob Geldof to put the show together.

It was later reported that Princess Diana, who attended the show with The Prince of Wales, had specifically requested to be introduced to David. Mick Jagger, with whom David duetted on a single and video of 'Dancing In The Street', the proceeds of which went to the Band Aid Trust, performed at the American Live Aid concert in Philadelphia later the same day. The audience was therefore denied the spectacle of Bowie and Jagger performing live together, although there was talk of the pair performing the song simultaneously – and therefore duetting – in both London and Philly. Technical problems eventually ruled out this ambitious plan.

It was a shame that Bowie chose to disband his Live Aid group after the show and, to date, not perform with them again. Judging by the quality of their performance – inspired, no doubt, by both the occasion and a wish to impress behind a colossus such as Bowie – they could have performed many concerts together, and the results might have been spectacular. In the event Bowie did not perform live again until 1987 apart from a Prince's Trust Show at Wembley Arena (when he *did* duet with Mick Jagger) before his chum The Princess of Wales in June 1986. (This was a spontaneous and largely unrehearsed appearance hastily arranged backstage where stars were hobnobbing with their friends. As a result their duet was not televised, unlike the appearances of other top stars, including show closer Paul McCartney.)

With the exception of his stunning performance at the Live Aid concert and simultaneous duet with Mick Jagger on a version of the old Vandellas' hit 'Dancing In The Street', David devoted much of 1985 to preparing himself for two upcoming film appearances, firstly 'Labyrinth', a sci-fi caper aimed primarily at children which would be directed by Muppets' creator Jim Henson, then the much-hyped movie of 'Absolute Beginners'.

'The David Bowie Collection'
Castle Communications CCSLP 118 double album. Released October 1985. Producers: Mike Vernon, Tony Hatch.
1. **The Laughing Gnome**
2. **Rubber Band**
3. **Love You Till Tuesday**
4. **Sell Me A Coat**
5. **In The Heat Of The Morning**
6. **Karma Man**
7. **Please Mr Gravedigger**
8. **The London Boys**
9. **She's Got Medals**
10. **Silly Boy Blue**
11. **Join The Gang**
12. **Did You Ever Have A Dream**
13. **The Gospel According To Tony Day**
14. **Can't Help Thinking About Me**
15. **And I Say To Myself**
16. **Do Anything You Say**
17. **Good Morning Girl**
18. **I Dig Everything**
19. **I'm Not Losing Sleep**
A reissue of Bowie's material on both Decca and Pye.

'The Falcon And The Snowman'
EMI America FAL 1. Released May 1985. Film soundtrack album. Includes one Bowie track produced by David Bowie and Pat Metheny.
This Is Not America (Bowie/Pat Metheny).

This Is Not America (extended)/**This Is Not America** (instrumental)
EMI America 12EA 190 12". Released March 1985.

Loving The Alien (remix) (Bowie)/**Don't Look Down** (remix) (Iggy Pop/James Williamson)
EMI America EA 195. Released May 1985.

(PHOTO: L.F.I.)

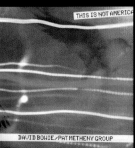

This Is Not America (Bowie/Pat Metheny)/**This Is Not America** (instrumental) (Bowie/Pat Metheny) EMI America EA 190. Released March 1985.

Loving The Alien (extended remix)/ **Don't Look Down** (remix) EMI America 12EA 195 12″. Released May 1985.

Loving The Alien (remix)/**Don't Look Down** (remix) EMI America EAP 195 picture disc. Released June 1985.

Loving The Alien (extended dance remix)/**Don't Look Down** (extended)/ **Loving The Alien** (dub) EMI America 12 EAP 196. Released June 1985.

I Pity The Fool (D.Malone)/**Take My Tip** (David Jones – alias Bowie)/**You've Got A Habit Of Leaving** (David Jones – Bowie)/**Baby Loves That Way** (Bowie) See For Miles SEA 1 12″. Released June 1985.

Dancing In The Street (with Mick Jagger) (Ivy Hunter/Micky Stevenson/ Marvin Gaye)/**Dancing In The Street** (instrumental) (Ivy Hunter/Micky Stevenson/Marvin Gaye EMI America EA 204. Released August 1985.

Dancing In The Street (with Mick Jagger) (Clearmountain mix)/**Dancing In The Street** (Steve Thompson mix)/ **Dancing In The Street** (dub)/**Dancing In The Street** (edit) EMI America 12EA 204 12″. Released August 1985.

DAVID AS THE GOBLIN KING IN LABYRINTH. (PHOTO: KOBAL COLLECTION)

'Labyrinth'
EMI America AML 3104. Released June 1986.
Film soundtrack album. Includes seven Bowie tracks, and six instrumental pieces by Terry Jones. Bowie material produced by David Bowie and Arif Mardin; album produced by David Bowie, Arif Mardin and Terry Jones.
1.　**Opening Titles** (Terry Jones, this includes brief portion of Underground, written by Bowie).
2.　**Magic Dance** (Bowie)
3.　**Sarah** (Bowie)
4.　**Chilly Down** (Bowie)
5.　**As The World Falls Down** (Bowie)
6.　**Within You** (Bowie)
7.　**Underground** (Bowie)

Absolute Beginners (Bowie)/**Absolute Beginners** (dub) (Bowie)
Virgin VS 838. Released March 1986.

'Absolute Beginners'
Virgin VD 2514 double album. Released April 1986.
Film soundtrack album. Includes three Bowie tracks produced by David Bowie, Clive Langer and Alan Winstanley, except Volare, produced by David Bowie and Erdal Kizilcay.
1.　**Absolute Beginners** (Bowie)
2.　**That's Motivation** (Bowie)
3.　**Volare** (Modungo/Migliacci)

Absolute Beginners (extended)/
Absolute Beginners (dub)
Virgin VS 12838 12". Released March 1986.

The London Boys (Bowie)/**Love You Till Tuesday** (Bowie)/**The Laughing Gnome** (Bowie)/**Maid Of Bond Street** (Bowie)
Archive 4 TOF 105 12" limited edition of 7,500. Released February 1986.

With this notable exception, 1986 was given over to filming. For 'Labyrinth' David adopted a hairstyle as strange as any since his days as Ziggy Stardust, all blond and spiky on top with long straight edges in the fashion preferred by less than tasteful heavy metal bands. He took the role of a Goblin King of dubious character, and also wrote five unexceptional songs for the film's soundtrack which, when released through EMI in June, was described by Melody Maker as 'under par music for under fives.' The film itself did not go on release until the following November.

'Absolute Beginners' was a far more extravagant affair, produced by Virgin Films, promoted beyond tolerance level but ideologically sound by virtue of Colin MacInnes' unquestionable street credibility with teenagers of the eighties. It was a musical – Bowie contributed a likeable title track – and that was perhaps where it failed despite all the hoopla that surrounded its release. Although the film's two central characters were portrayed by Eddie O'Connell and easy-on-the-eye nymphette Patsy Kensit, Bowie, as the biggest celebrity involved, was wheeled out to give interviews to promote the film. 'The nearest thing I can think of to ('Absolute Beginners') is 'Guys And Dolls',' he told Today. 'It's really quite extraordinary. It's very stylised. Everything's a little bit larger than life. It doesn't go into a video-type number at all. It doesn't have that look. It's much more of a fifties 'Singing In The Rain' feel. I have a dance routine which is going to blow my cool even more . . . it's a tap dance.'

Elsewhere during the same interview David was critical of the current music scene ('Oh the music is so awful here . . . it's absolutely dreadful') and dismissive of the controversial book 'Alias David Bowie' which was previewed in The Sunday Times. 'When they drag out long lost aunts to supply all the details, aunts I've had absolutely no contact with for maybe 20 years – who have no knowledge of me – and absolutely unbelievable, blatant lies are told . . .'

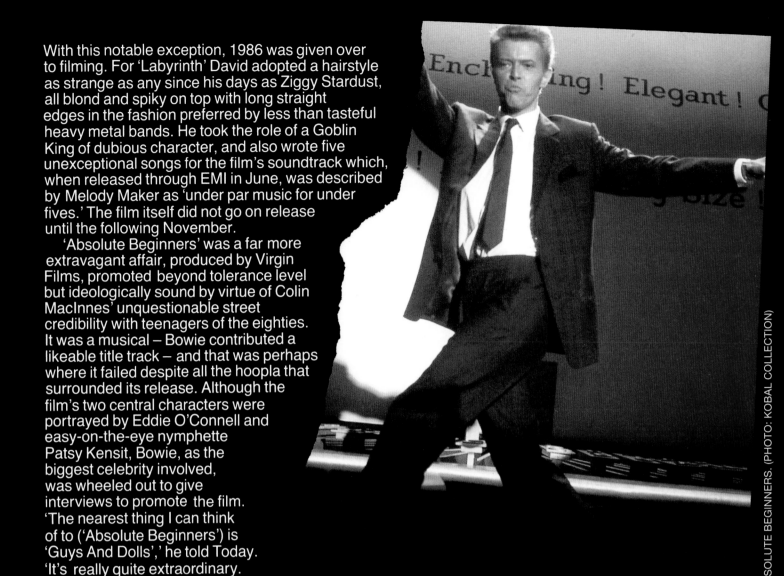

DAVID IN ABSOLUTE BEGINNERS. (PHOTO: KOBAL COLLECTION)

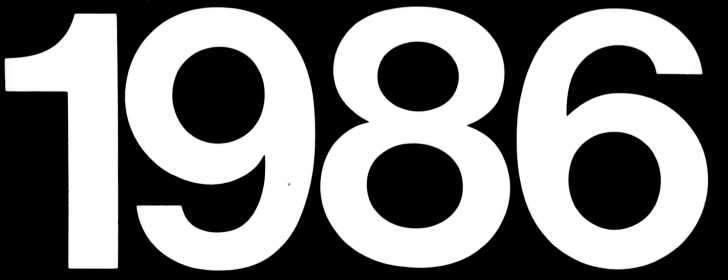

1986

DAVID WITH PETER FRAMPTON ON THE GLASS SPIDER TOUR. (PHOTO: L.F.I.)

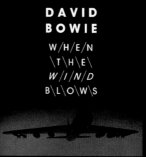

DAVID BOWIE

W/H/E/N
\T\H\E\
W/I/N/D
B\L\O\W\S

'Absolute Beginners'
Virgin V 2386. Released March 1986.
Film soundtrack album. Includes two
Bowie tracks produced by David Bowie,
Clive Langer and Alan Winstanley.
1. **Absolute Beginners** (Bowie).
2. **That's Motivation** (Bowie).

Absolute Beginners/Absolute Beginners (dub)
Virgin VSS 838 picture disc. Released
March 1986.

Underground (Bowie)/**Underground**
(instrumental) (Bowie)
EMI America EA 216. Released June
1986.

Underground (extended)/
Underground (instrumental)
EMI America 12EA 216 12". Released
June 1986.

When The Wind Blows (Bowie)/**When The Wind Blows** (dub) (Bowie)
Virgin VS 906. Released October 1986.

When The Wind Blows (extended)/
When The Wind Blows (dub)
Virgin VS 906-12 12". Released October 1986.

Never Let Me Down'
EMI America AMLS 3117. Released April 1987.
Producers: David Bowie and David Richards.

1. **Day In Day Out** (Bowie)
2. **Time Will Crawl** (Bowie)
3. **Beat Of Your Heart** (Bowie)
4. **Never Let Me Down** (Bowie/Carlos Alomar)
5. **Zeroes** (Bowie)
6. **Glass Spider** (Bowie)

8. **New York's In Love** (Bowie)
9. **'87 And Cry** (Bowie)
10. **Too Dizzy** (Bowie/Erdal Kizilcay)
11. **Bang Bang** (Iggy Pop/Ivan Kral)

Carlos Alomar: Guitar, Guitar synthesizer.
Erdal Kizilcay: Keyboards, Drums, Bass, Trumpet.
Peter Frampton: Lead guitar.
Carmine Rojas: Additional bass.
Phillipe Saisse: Piano.
Crusher Bennett: Percussion.
Laurie Frink: Trumpet
Earl Gardner: Trumpet, Flugelhorn.
Stan Harrison, Steve Elson, Lenny Pickett: The Borneo Horns
Robin Clark, Loni Groves, Diva Gray, Gordon Grodie and the Coquettes – Coco, Sandro, Charuvan, Joe, Clement, John, Aglae: Vocals.

(PHOTO: L.F.I.)

Time Will Crawl (extended)/**Girls**
(extended)
EMI America 12EA 237 12″. Released
April 1987.

Day In Day Out (Bowie)/**Julie** (Bowie)
EMI America EA 230. Released March
1987.

Day In Day Out (extended dance mix)/
Day In Day Out (extended dub mix)/
Julie
EMI America 12EA 230 12″. Released
March 1987.

Never Let Me Down/Time Will Crawl
(extended dance mix)/**Day In Day Out**
(Groucho mix)
EMI America PCEA 239 cassette single.
Released August 1987.

It is doubtful whether 1987 will go down as a vintage Bowie year in the minds of his supporters. He chose to tour expansively and extensively in order to promote his next album 'Don't Let Me Down' but ambitious staging, questionable choice of material and an over-reliance on special effects left many disappointed. Commercially successful it may have been, but the critics savaged Bowie throughout the year, firstly on the weakness of the LP and secondly on the blandness of his concerts.

The Bowie year began in March when David hosted a press conference at the Players Theatre underneath the arches at Charing Cross. He also performed his new single 'Day-In Day-Out', much to the delight of a few stray fans who'd been invited inside by David himself. His latest band included Peter Frampton, a fellow alumni of Bromley Technical High School, as well as loyal trooper Carlos Alomar.

Question time began with Bowie fending off enquiries concerning whether or not this would be his 'farewell tour'. 'I never said that I was retiring,' he told the throng, evidently referring to an item in that day's Daily Star. 'And I didn't say the show would feature costumes, make-up and sex . . . I said it would feature costumes, make-up and theatrical sets.' 'Yes, I've taken an AIDS test,' he replied when the topic -on-everyone's-lips was mentioned. 'I would do so every time I change a partner and I would suggest everyone else does the same. I also suggest they wear condoms. It's one of the most frightening diseases this planet has ever faced. I have absolutely no plans to marry at the moment but you never know, do you?' On the subject of his soon-to-be-released LP Bowie said: 'I wrote the album over a three-month period before I started recording. It's very high energy compared to previous albums and very orientated to being in a small band on stage. The pivotal song on the album is 'Glass Spiders'. Spiders keep coming up in my references all the time. I don't know what the Jungian aspects of it are but I see them as some kind of mother figure . . .'

The Glass Spider stage was technically more complex than any DB had ever performed upon before, including even the elaborate Diamond Dogs Revue package which never toured outside of North America. Three separate stages were built, each focused around a 60-foot spider, and 43

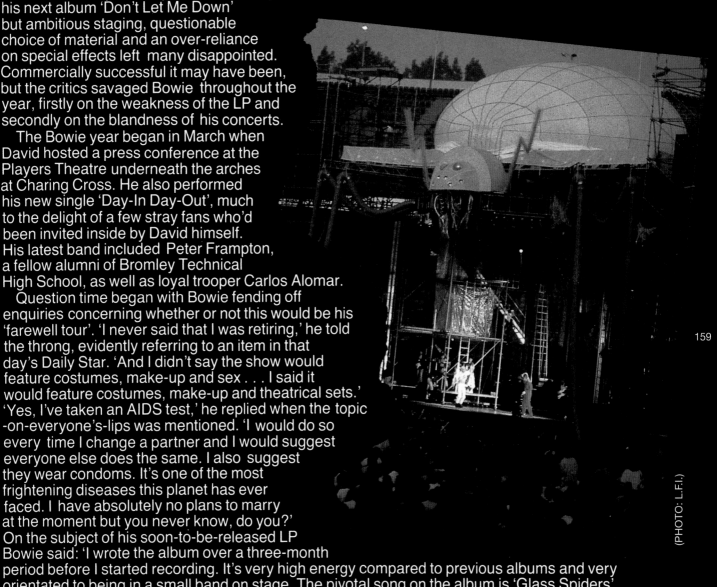

159

(PHOTO: L.F.I.)

1987

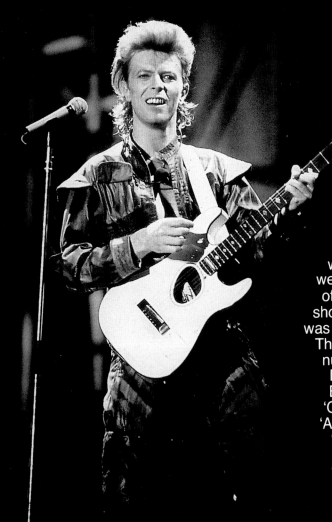

trucks were required to ensure they reached their destinations on time. There was 600,000 watts of lighting power in use, gantries that supported the star and held him aloft like Caesar bestowing laurels, and 150 personnel were on hand to keep the show on the road. The London press conference was one of eight that Bowie conducted during March; Toronto, New York, Paris, Madrid, Rome, Munich and Amsterdam were also favoured. The tour proper opened in May, in Rotterdam, and moved across Europe during June and July. North American dates followed in the autumn. In London David performed two concerts at Wembley Stadium on June 19 and 20, and the weather was as unkind to the fans as the critics were to the star of the show. Not even the presence of the admiring Princess Diana, who attended both shows, could stem the wind and rain during what was actually the wettest June on record for many years. The basic song set for the tour comprised 25 numbers including encores, with the 'Never Let Me Down' album tracks strongly featured. 'Up The Hill Backwards' was the regular opener, followed by 'Glass Spider','Day-In Day-Out', 'Bang Bang', 'Absolute Beginners', 'Loving The Alien', 'China Girl', 'Fashion', 'Scary Monsters', 'All The Madmen', 'Never Let Me Down', 'Big Brother', '87 And Cry', 'Heroes', 'Time Will Crawl', 'Beat On Your Drum', 'Sons Of The Silent Age', 'New York's In Love', 'Zeroes', 'Dancing With Big Boys', 'Let's Dance' and 'Fame'. The encores were generally 'Time', 'Blue Jean' and 'Modern Love'.

The American leg of the tour which followed later in the year was marred by an incident following the concert in Dallas, Texas, in October, when 30-year-old Wanda Nicholls claimed that Bowie had raped her in his hotel suite. When the case subsequently went to court the charges were thrown out, the likeliest outcome of what appeared to be a clear case of self-publicity seeking.

With the tour over Bowie again disappeared from the public view to contemplate his future amid the slings and arrows that 1987 had brought. There was little reason for serious concern, though it seems unlikely that he will emerge from his shell for another concert tour in the near future . . . but when that time comes how refreshing it would be to see Bowie on stage without gargantuan props and complex staging, performing with a band of young and eager-to-please musicians like those who backed him at Live Aid. Back to basics is the best way to go.

Day In Day Out (extended remix)/**Day In Day Out** (extended dub mix)/**Julie**
EMI America 12EAX 230 12″. Released April 1987.

Time Will Crawl (Bowie)/**Girls** (Bowie)
EMI America EA 237. Released April 1987.

Never Let Me Down (Bowie/Carlos Alomar)/**87 And Cry** (Bowie)
EMI America EA 239. Released August 1987.

Never Let Me Down (extended remix)/
87 And Cry (extended)
EMI America 12EA 239 12″. Released August 1987.

'David Bowie'
PRT PYL 6001. Released October 1987.
Producer: Tony Hatch.
1. **I'm Not Losing Sleep**
2. **I Dig Everything**
3. **Can't Help Thinking About Me**
4. **Do Anything You Say**
5. **Good Morning Girl**
6. **And I Say To Myself**
A re-issue of Bowie's material on Pye Records.